W9-CPL-854

Quick & Easy
Chicken Dishes

p

Contents

Introduction

Chicken has become justly popular around the world and plays an important part in the modern diet, being reasonably priced and nutritionally sound. A versatile meat, it lends itself to an ample range of cooking methods and cuisines. Its unassertive flavor means that it is equally suited to cooking with sweet and savory flavors. Because it has a low fat content, especially without the skin, it is an ideal meat for low cholesterol and calorie-controlled diets. An excellent source of protein, chicken contains valuable minerals, such as potassium and phosphorus, and some of the B vitamins.

Cooking Methods for Chicken

Roasting Remove any fat from the body cavity. Rinse the bird inside and out with water, then pat dry with paper towels. Season the cavity generously with salt and pepper, and add stuffing, or herbs. Spread the breast with softened butter or oil. Set on a rack in a roasting pan or a shallow baking dish. Roast the bird, basting two or three times with the pan juices during roasting. If the chicken is browning too quickly, cover it with foil. Test that it is cooked as described in Food Safety & Tips, opposite. Put the bird on a carving board and let rest for at least 15 minutes before serving. Make a sauce from the juices left in the roasting pan.

Broiling A broiler's intense heat quickly seals the flesh beneath a crisp exterior. Place the chicken 4–6 inches/ 10–15 cm from a moderate heat source. If it browns too quickly, reduce the heat slightly. If the chicken is broiled too near the heat at too high a temperature, the outside will burn before the inside is cooked. If it is cooked for too long under a low heat, it will dry out. Divide the chicken into joints to ensure even cooking. Breast meat, if cooked in one piece, can be dry, so it is best to cut it into chunks. Wings are best for fast broiling.

Deep-Frying This is suitable for small drumsticks, thighs, and joints. Dry the chicken pieces with paper towels to prevent spitting and so that they brown properly. The chicken may be coated in seasoned flour, egg, and bread crumbs, or a batter. Heat

a little oil or a mixture of oil and butter in a heavy skillet. When the oil is very hot, add the chicken pieces, skin-side down. Cook until golden brown all over, turning frequently. Drain well on paper towels before serving.

Sautéeing This is ideal for small pieces or small birds, such as squabs Heat a little oil or a mixture of oil and butter in a heavy skillet. Add the chicken and cook over a moderate heat until golden brown, turning frequently. Add bouillon or other liquid, bring to a boil, then cover and reduce the heat. Cook gently until cooked through.

Stir-frying Skinless, boneless chicken is cut into small pieces of equal size to ensure that the meat cooks evenly and stays succulent. Preheat a wok or a pan before adding a small amount of oil. When the oil starts to smoke, add the chicken and stir-fry with your chosen flavorings for 3–4 minutes, or until cooked through. Other ingredients can be cooked at the same time, or the chicken can be cooked by itself, then removed from the pan while you stir-fry the remaining ingredients. Return the chicken to the pan once the other ingredients are cooked.

Casseroling This method is the best one for cooking joints from larger, more mature chickens, although smaller chickens can be cooked whole. The slow cooking produces tender meat with a good flavor. Brown the chicken in butter or oil or a mixture of both. Add

bouillon, wine, or a mixture of both, with seasonings and herbs, then cover and cook on top of the stove or in the oven until the chicken is tender. Add lightly sautéed vegetables about halfway through the cooking time.

Braising This method does not involve adding liquid. Chicken pieces or a small whole chicken with vegetables are cooked at a low temperature in a preheated oven. Heat a little oil in an ovenproof and flameproof casserole, and gently cook the chicken until it is golden. Remove it and cook the vegetables until they are almost tender. Replace the chicken, cover tightly, and cook gently on the top of the stove or in an oven at a low temperature until chicken and vegetables are tender.

Poaching This gentle method produces tender chicken and a bouillon. Put a whole chicken, a bouquet garni, a leek, a carrot, and an onion in a large flameproof casserole. Cover with water, season, and bring to a boil. Cover and simmer for 1½–2 hours, or until the chicken is tender. Lift it out, discard the bouquet garni, use the bouillon to make a sauce, and blend the vegetables to thicken the bouillon, or serve them with the chicken.

Food Safety & Tips

Chicken is liable to be contaminated by salmonella bacteria, which can cause severe food poisoning. When storing, handling, and preparing poultry, it is vital to observe the following precautions to prevent illness:
1. Check the "use-by" date and the "best before" date. After buying, take the chicken home quickly, preferably in a freezer bag or a cool box.
2. Place birds bought frozen in the freezer immediately.
3. To store in the refrigerator, remove wrappings and store giblets separately. Place the chicken in a shallow dish to catch drips. Cover loosely with foil and store on the bottom shelf for no more than two or three days, depending on the "best before" date. Avoid contact between raw chicken and cooked food during storage and preparation. Wash your hands thoroughly after handling raw chicken.
4. Prepare raw chicken on a chopping board that can be easily cleaned, such as a nonporous, plastic board.

5. Frozen birds should be defrosted before cooking. If time permits, defrost in the refrigerator for about 36 hours, or thaw for about 12 hours in a cool place. The flesh should feel soft and flexible, with no ice crystals. Bacteria breed in chicken thawing to room temperature. Cooking at high temperatures kills them, so cook the chicken as soon as possible after thawing.
6. Test that chicken is cooked thoroughly by using a meat thermometer. The thigh should reach at least 175°F/79°C when cooked. Alternatively, pierce the thickest part of a thigh with a skewer, and the juices should run clear, not pink or red. Never partially cook chicken with the intention of completing cooking later.

Chicken Bouillon

A well-flavored chicken bouillon is made from a whole bird, or the wings, carcass, and legs. A bouillon made from just chicken bones cooked with vegetables and flavorings will be less rich. A simple bouillon can be made from giblets (not the liver, which is bitter) with a bouquet garni, onion, carrot, and peppercorns. Home-made bouillon can be stored in the freezer for up to six months.

To make chicken bouillon: place a whole chicken or wings and carcass in a large pan with two quartered onions. Cook until the chicken and onion are evenly browned. Cover with cold water, bring to a boil, and skim off any scum from the surface. Add two chopped carrots, two chopped celery stalks, a small bunch of parsley, a few bay leaves, a thyme sprig, and a few peppercorns. Partially cover and simmer for about 3 hours. Strain the bouillon into a bowl, let cool, then refrigerate. When it is cold, remove the fat that will have set on the surface.

KEY

🐾 Simplicity level 1 – 3 (1 easiest, 3 slightly harder)

🍖 Preparation time

🕐 Cooking time

Cream of Chicken Soup

Tarragon adds a delicate aniseed flavor to this tasty soup. If you cannot find tarragon, use parsley for a fresh taste.

NUTRITIONAL INFORMATION

Calories	420	Sugars	.........4g
Protein	.......24g	Fat	.........33g
Carbohydrate	....6g	Saturates	......20g

10 mins   25 mins

SERVES 4

INGREDIENTS

4 tbsp unsalted butter

1 large onion, chopped

10½ oz/300 g cooked chicken, shredded finely

2½ cups chicken bouillon

1 tbsp chopped fresh tarragon

⅔ cup heavy cream

salt and pepper

fresh tarragon leaves, to garnish

deep-fried croûtons, to serve

1   Melt the butter in a large saucepan and fry the onion for 3 minutes.

2   Add the finely shredded chicken to the saucepan together with 1¼ cups of the chicken bouillon. Mix the ingredients together in the pan.

3   Bring to a boil and simmer for 20 minutes. Let cool, then mix the soup using a blender.

4   Add the remainder of the bouillon and season with salt and pepper.

5   Add the chopped tarragon. Pour the soup into a tureen or individual serving bowls and add a swirl of cream.

6   Garnish the soup with fresh tarragon and serve with deep-fried croûtons.

VARIATION

If you can't find fresh tarragon, freeze-dried tarragon makes a good substitute. Light cream can be used instead of the heavy cream to reduce the calorie content.

Tom's Chicken Soup

The potato has been part of the Irish diet for centuries. This recipe came originally from Moira, County Down, Northern Ireland.

NUTRITIONAL INFORMATION

Calories	97	Sugars	.......1.8g
Protein	........7.3g	Fat	..........2g
Carbohydrate	...4.2g	Saturates	.....3.3g

10 mins   1 hr 15 mins

SERVES 4

INGREDIENTS

3 smoked, streaky, rindless bacon slices, chopped

1 lb 2 oz/500 g boneless chicken, chopped

2 tbsp butter

3 potatoes, chopped

3 onions, chopped

2½ cups giblet or chicken bouillon

2½ cups milk

salt and pepper

⅔ cup heavy cream

2 tbsp chopped fresh parsley

soda bread, to serve

1 Gently fry the bacon and chicken in a large saucepan for 10 minutes.

2 Add the butter, potatoes, and onions and cook for 15 minutes, stirring all the time.

3 Add the bouillon and milk, then bring to a boil and simmer for 45 minutes. Season with salt and pepper to taste.

4 Blend in the cream and simmer the soup for 5 minutes. Stir in the chopped fresh parsley, then transfer the soup to a warm tureen or individual bowls and serve with soda bread.

VARIATION

For a more filling, main course soup, you can add any number of different vegetables, for example leeks, celery root, or corn.

Vegetable & Garbanzo Soup

A tasty soup, full of vegetables, chicken, and garbanzo beans, with just a hint of spiciness, to serve on any occasion.

NUTRITIONAL INFORMATION

Calories	271	Sugar	. . . . .6g
Protein	. . . . .17g	Fats	. . . . .13g
Carbohydrates	. . .24g	Saturates	. . . . . .2g

10 mins   55 mins

SERVES 4–6

I N G R E D I E N T S

3 tbsp olive oil

1 large onion, finely chopped

2–3 garlic cloves, crushed

½–1 red chile, deseeded and very finely chopped

1 skinless, boneless chicken breast (about 5½ oz/150 g), sliced thickly

2 celery stalks, chopped finely

6 oz/175 g carrots, grated coarsely

5¾ cups chicken bouillon

2 bay leaves

½ tsp dried oregano

¼ tsp ground cinnamon

14 oz/400 g can of garbanzo beans, drained

2 tomatoes, peeled, deseeded, and chopped

1 tbsp tomato paste

salt and pepper

chopped fresh cilantro or parsley, to garnish

corn or wheat tortillas, to serve

1 Heat the oil in a large saucepan and fry the onion, garlic and chile very gently until they are softened but not colored.

2 Add the chicken to the saucepan and continue to cook until well sealed and lightly browned.

3 Add the celery, carrots, bouillon, bay leaves, oregano, cinnamon, and salt and pepper. Bring to a boil, then cover and simmer gently for about 20 minutes, or until the chicken is tender and cooked throughout.

4 Remove the chicken from the soup and chop it finely, or cut it into narrow strips.

5 Return the chicken to the pan with the garbanzo beans, tomatoes, and tomato paste. Simmer, covered, for another 15–20 minutes. Discard the bay leaves, then adjust the seasoning.

6 Serve very hot sprinkled with parsley or cilantro and accompanied by warmed tortillas.

Chicken Consommé

This is a very flavorful soup, especially if you make it from real chicken bouillon. Egg shells are used to give a crystal clear appearance.

NUTRITIONAL INFORMATION

Calories	96	Sugars	.........1g
Protein	........11g	Fat	...........1g
Carbohydrate	....1g	Saturates	.....0.4g

10 mins   55 mins

SERVES 4

I N G R E D I E N T S

7½ cups chicken bouillon

⅔ cup medium sherry

4 egg whites, plus egg shells

4¼ oz/125 g cooked lean chicken, sliced thinly

salt and pepper

1 Place the chicken bouillon and sherry in a large saucepan and heat gently for 5 minutes.

2 Add the egg whites and the egg shells to the chicken bouillon and whisk until the mixture begins to boil.

3 When the mixture boils, remove the pan from the heat and let the mixture subside for 10 minutes. Repeat this process three times. This lets the egg white trap the sediments in the chicken bouillon to clarify the soup.

4 Let the chicken consommé cool for 5 minutes.

5 Carefully place a piece of fine cheesecloth over a clean saucepan. Ladle the soup over the cheesecloth and strain the liquid into the saucepan.

6 Repeat this process twice, then gently reheat the consommé. Season with salt and pepper to taste, then add the chicken slices to the consommé and serve immediately.

COOK'S TIP

For extra color, add a garnish to the soup. Use a tablespoon each of finely diced carrot, celery, and turnip, or some finely chopped herbs, such as parsley or tarragon.

Chicken & Rice Soup

This soup is a good way of using up leftover cooked chicken and rice. Any type of rice is suitable, from white or brown long-grain rice to wild rice.

NUTRITIONAL INFORMATION

Calories	165	Sugars	.........3g
Protein	........14g	Fat	...........4g
Carbohydrate	...19g	Saturates	.......1g

5 mins 30 mins

SERVES 4

INGREDIENTS

6¾ cups chicken bouillon (see Cook's Tip)

2 small carrots, very thinly sliced

1 celery stalk, finely diced

1 baby leek, halved lengthwise and thinly sliced

4 oz/115 g tiny peas, defrosted if frozen

3 cups cooked rice

5½ oz/150 g cooked chicken, sliced

2 tsp chopped fresh tarragon

1 tbsp chopped fresh parsley

salt and pepper

fresh parsley sprigs, to garnish

1 Pour the bouillon into a large saucepan and add the carrots, celery, and leek. Bring to a boil, then reduce the heat to low and simmer the bouillon gently, partially covered, for 10 minutes.

2 Stir in the peas, rice, and chicken, and continue cooking for another 10–15 minutes, or until the vegetables are tender.

3 Add the chopped tarragon and parsley, then taste and adjust the seasoning, adding salt and pepper as needed.

4 Ladle the soup into warm bowls, garnish with parsley and serve.

COOK'S TIP

If the bouillon you are using is a little on the weak side, or if you have used a bouillon cube, add the herbs at the beginning, so that they can flavor the bouillon for a longer time.

Thai Coconut Soup

This soup makes a change from traditional chicken soup. It is spicy, and garnished with a generous quantity of fresh cilantro leaves.

NUTRITIONAL INFORMATION

Calories 76	Sugars 2g
Protein 13g	Fat 1g
Carbohydrate 3g	Saturates 0g

5 mins   40 mins

SERVES 4

INGREDIENTS

5 cups chicken bouillon

7 oz/200 g skinless boned chicken

1 fresh chile, split lengthwise
  and deseeded

3 inch/7.5 cm piece lemon grass,
  split lengthwise

3–4 lime leaves

1 inch/2.5 cm piece fresh ginger root,
  peeled and sliced

½ cup coconut milk

6–8 scallions, sliced diagonally

¼ tsp chili paste, to taste

salt

fresh cilantro leaves, to garnish

1 Put the bouillon in a pan with the chicken, chile, lemon grass, lime leaves, and ginger. Bring almost to a boil, reduce the heat, cover and simmer for 20–25 minutes, or until the chicken is cooked through and firm to the touch.

2 Remove the chicken from the pan and strain the bouillon. When the chicken is cool, slice thinly, or shred into bite-sized pieces.

3 Return the bouillon to the saucepan and heat to simmering. Stir in the coconut milk and scallions. Add the chicken and continue simmering for about 10 minutes, or until the soup is heated through and the flavors have mingled.

4 Stir in the chili paste. Season to taste with salt and, if wished, add a little more chili paste.

5 Ladle into warm bowls and float cilantro leaves on top to serve.

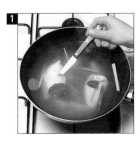

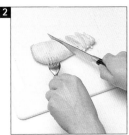

COOK'S TIP

Once the bouillon is flavored and the chicken cooked, this soup is very quick to finish. If you wish, poach the chicken and strain the bouillon ahead of time. Store in the refrigerator separately.

Lemon & Chicken Soup

This delicately flavored summer soup is surprisingly easy to make and may be prepared well in advance of its serving time.

NUTRITIONAL INFORMATION

Calories	506	Sugars	.........4g
Protein	........19g	Fat	..........31g
Carbohydrate	...41g	Saturates	......19g

🥔 10 mins   🕐 1 hr 10 mins

SERVES 4

INGREDIENTS

4 tbsp butter

8 shallots, thinly sliced

2 carrots, thinly sliced

2 celery stalks, thinly sliced

8 oz/225 g boned chicken breasts,chopped

3 lemons, thinly pared and juiced, with
    slices reserved for garnish

5 cups chicken bouillon

8 oz/225 g dried spaghetti, broken into
    small pieces

salt and white pepper

⅔ cup heavy cream

TO GARNISH

fresh parsley sprig

3 lemon slices, halved

1 Melt the butter in a large pan. Add the shallots, carrots, celery, and chicken and cook over a low heat for 8 minutes.

2 Pare the lemons thinly, blanch the rind in boiling water for 3 minutes. Squeeze the lemons and keep the juice.

3 Add the lemon zest and juice to the pan, with the bouillon. Bring slowly to a boil over a low heat, and simmer for 40 minutes, stirring occasionally.

4 Add the spaghetti to the pan and cook for 15 minutes. Season, and add the cream. Heat through, but do not let the soup boil or it will curdle.

5 Pour the soup into a tureen. Serve immediately, garnished with parsley.

COOK'S TIP

You can prepare this soup up to the end of step 3 in advance, so that all you need do before serving is heat it through before adding the pasta and the finishing touches.

Avocado & Chipotle Soup

This soup evolved from the street food stalls of Mexico City. Rich avocado, shreds of chicken, and the smoky hit of chipotle make it special.

NUTRITIONAL INFORMATION

Calories 218   Sugars 1g
Protein . . . . .28g   Fat 11g
Carbohydrate . . . .2g   Saturates 2g

15 mins   5 mins

SERVES 4

INGREDIENTS

6¾ cups chicken bouillon

2–3 garlic cloves, finely chopped

1–2 chipotle chilis, cut into very thin strips (see Cook's Tip)

1 avocado, diced

lime or lemon juice, for tossing

3–5 scallions, thinly sliced

12–14 oz/350–400 g cooked chicken breast, torn or cut into shreds or thin strips

2 tbsp chopped fresh cilantro

TO SERVE

1 lime, cut into wedges

handful of tortilla chips, optional

1 Place the bouillon in a pan with the garlic and chipotle chilis and bring to a boil.

2 Meanwhile, cut the avocado in half around the large stone. Twist apart, then remove the stone with a knife. Carefully peel off the skin, dice the flesh, then toss in the citrus juice to prevent the fruit discoloring.

3 Arrange the thinly sliced scallions, the cooked chicken, diced avocado, and the fresh cilantro equally in the bases of 4 soup bowls or in a single large serving bowl.

4 Ladle the hot bouillon over the arrangement, and serve with the wedges of lime and a handful of tortilla chips, if using.

COOK'S TIP

Chipotle chilis are smoked and dried jalapeño chiles, available canned or dried from specialist stores. Use those canned in adobo marinade for this recipe, if possible. Drain the canned chipotles before using. Dried chipotles need to be reconstituted before use.

Chicken & Bean Soup

This hearty and nourishing soup, combining garbanzo beans and chicken, is an ideal appetizer for a family supper, or it can make a snack on its own.

NUTRITIONAL INFORMATION

Calories	347	Sugars	.........2g
Protein	........28g	Fat	..........11g
Carbohydrate	...37g	Saturates	.......4g

15 mins

2 hrs 30 mins

SERVES 4

INGREDIENTS

2 tbsp butter

3 scallions, chopped

2 garlic cloves, crushed

1 fresh marjoram sprig, finely chopped

12 oz/350 g boned chicken breasts, diced

5 cups chicken bouillon

12 oz/350 g can garbanzo beans, drained

1 bouquet garni sachet

1 red bell pepper, diced

1 green bell pepper, diced

4 oz/115 g small dried pasta shapes, such as elbow macaroni

salt and white pepper

croûtons, to serve

COOK'S TIP

If you prefer, you can use dried garbanzo beans. Cover with cold water and set aside to soak for 5–8 hours. Drain and add the beans to the soup, according to the recipe, and allow an additional 30 minutes–1 hour cooking time.

1 Melt the butter in a large saucepan. Add the scallions, garlic, sprig of fresh marjoram, and the diced chicken and cook, stirring frequently, over a medium heat for 5 minutes.

2 Add the chicken bouillon, garbanzo beans, and bouquet garni sachet, then season with salt and white pepper.

3 Bring the soup to a boil, then lower the heat and simmer for about 2 hours.

4 Add the diced bell peppers and pasta shapes to the pan, then simmer for another 20 minutes.

5 Transfer the soup to a warm tureen. To serve, ladle the soup into individual serving bowls and serve immediately, garnished with the croûtons.

Chicken Balls with Sauce

Serve these bite-sized chicken appetizers warm as a snack, with drinks, or packed cold for a picnic or a lunchbox treat.

NUTRITIONAL INFORMATION

Calories 214	Sugars 29g	
Protein 20g	Fat 13g	
Carbohydrate 5g	Saturates 2g	

🍲 10 mins   🕐 20 mins

SERVES 4

I N G R E D I E N T S

2 large boneless, skinless chicken breasts

3 tbsp vegetable oil

2 shallots, finely chopped

1/2 celery stalk, finely chopped

1 garlic clove, crushed

2 tbsp light soy sauce

1 small egg

salt and pepper

1 bunch scallions

scallion tassels, to garnish

D I P P I N G   S A U C E

3 tbsp dark soy sauce

1 tbsp rice wine

1 tsp sesame seeds

1 Cut the chicken into ³/₄ inch/2 cm pieces. Heat half of the oil in a skillet or wok and stir-fry the chicken over a high heat for 2–3 minutes, or until golden. Remove from the pan with a perforated spoon; set aside.

2 Add the shallots, celery, and garlic to the pan and stir-fry for 1–2 minutes until softened but not browned.

3 Place the chicken, shallots, celery, and garlic in a food processor and process until finely ground. Add 1 tablespoon of the light soy sauce, just enough egg to make a fairly firm mixture, and then add salt and pepper.

4 Trim the scallions and then cut into 2 inch/5 cm lengths. Make the dipping sauce by mixing together the dark soy sauce, rice wine, and sesame seeds, then set aside.

5 Shape the chicken mixture into 16–18 walnut-sized balls. Heat the remaining oil in the skillet or wok and then stir-fry the balls in small batches for 4–5 minutes, or until they are golden brown. As each batch is cooked drain on paper towels and keep hot.

6 Stir-fry the scallions for 1–2 minutes until they just begin to soften, then stir in the remaining light soy sauce. Serve this together with the hot chicken balls and a bowl of dipping sauce on a serving platter, garnished with the scallion tassels.

Chicken & Asparagus Soup

This light, clear soup has a delicate flavor of asparagus and freshly picked herbs. Use a good quality bouillon for best results.

NUTRITIONAL INFORMATION

Calories	224	Sugars	........2g
Protein	........27g	Fat	..........5g
Carbohydrate	...12g	Saturates	......1g

🕒 5 mins   ⏰ 15 mins

SERVES 4

INGREDIENTS

8 oz/225 g fresh asparagus

3½ cups fresh chicken bouillon (see page 5)

⅔ cup dry white wine

1 sprig each fresh parsley, dill, and tarragon

1 garlic clove

2¼ oz/60 g vermicelli rice noodles

12 oz/350 g cooked lean chicken, finely shredded

salt and white pepper

1 small leek, finely shredded

1 Wash the asparagus and trim away the woody ends. Cut each spear into pieces 1½ inches/4 cm long.

2 Pour the bouillon and wine into a large saucepan and bring to a boil.

3 Wash the herbs and tie them with clean string. Peel the garlic clove and add, with the herbs, to the saucepan together with the asparagus and noodles. Cover and simmer for 5 minutes.

4 Stir in the chicken and plenty of seasoning. Simmer gently for another 3–4 minutes, or until heated through.

5 Trim the leek, slice it down the center, then wash under running water to remove any dirt. Shake dry and shred finely.

6 Remove the herbs and garlic from the pan and discard. Ladle the soup into warm bowls, sprinkle with shredded leek and serve at once.

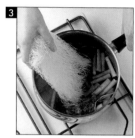

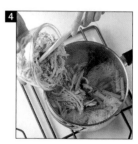

VARIATION

You can use any of your favorite herbs in this recipe, but choose those with a subtle flavor so that they do not overpower the asparagus. Small, tender asparagus spears give the best results and flavor.

Chicken & Leek Soup

This satisfying soup may be served as a main course. Add rice and bell peppers to make it even more hearty, and colorful.

NUTRITIONAL INFORMATION

Calories	183	Sugar	.........4g
Protein	........21g	Fats	...........9g
Carbohydrates	....4g	Saturates	......5g

5 mins · 1¼ hrs, plus 20 mins for rice

SERVES 4–6

I N G R E D I E N T S

2 tbsp butter

12 oz/350 g leeks

12 oz/350 g boneless chicken

5 cups fresh chicken bouillon (see page 5)

1 bouquet garni sachet

8 pitted prunes, halved

salt and white pepper

½ cup cooked rice and diced bell peppers, optional

1 Melt the butter in a large saucepan. Cut the leeks into 1 inch/2.5 cm pieces.

2 Add the chicken and leeks to the saucepan and fry for 8 minutes.

3 Next add the chicken bouillon and bouquet garni sachet and stir together well.

4 Season the mixture well with salt and freshly ground pepper to taste.

5 Bring the Chicken and Leek Soup to a boil and simmer for 45 minutes.

6 Add the pitted prunes to the saucepan with the cooked rice and diced bell peppers, if using, and simmer for about 20 minutes.

7 Remove the bouquet garni sachet from the soup and discard. Serve the soup immediately.

VARIATION

Instead of the bouquet garni sachet, you can use a bunch of fresh mixed herbs, tied together with string. Choose herbs such as parsley, thyme, and rosemary.

Chicken & Ham Pâté

Pâté is easy to make at home, and this combination of lean chicken and ham mixed with herbs is especially straightforward.

NUTRITIONAL INFORMATION

Calories	119	Sugars	........2g
Protein	........20g	Fat	..........3g
Carbohydrate	....2g	Saturates	......1g

🍲 10 mins 🕐 30 mins

SERVES 4

INGREDIENTS

8 oz/225 g cooked, lean, skinless chicken

3½ oz/100 g lean ham, trimmed

small bunch fresh parsley

1 tsp lime zest, grated

2 tbsp lime juice

1 garlic clove, peeled

¹⁄₂ cup low-fat, natural, unsweetened yoghurt

salt and pepper

1 tsp lime zest, to garnish

TO SERVE

lime wedges

crisp bread

green salad

1 Dice the chicken and ham and place in a blender or food processor.

2 Add the parsley, the lime zest and juice, and garlic to the chicken and ham, and process well until finely ground. Alternatively, finely chop the chicken, ham, parsley, and garlic and place in a bowl. Mix gently with the lime zest and juice.

3 Transfer the mixture to a bowl and mix in the unsweetened yoghurt. Season with salt and pepper to taste. Cover and let chill in the refrigerator for about 30 minutes.

4 Pile the pâté into individual serving dishes and garnish with lime zest. Serve the pâtés with lime wedges, crisp bread, and a fresh green salad.

VARIATION

This pâté can be made successfully with other kinds of ground, lean, cooked meat such as turkey, beef, and pork. Alternatively, replace the meat with peeled shrimp and/or white crab meat, or with canned tuna in brine, drained.

Sticky Ginger Chicken Wings

A finger-licking appetizer of chicken wings or drumsticks which is ideal for parties (have finger bowls ready).

NUTRITIONAL INFORMATION

Calories 416   Sugars 5g
Protein . . . . .41g   Fat 25g
Carbohydrate . . . .7g   Saturates 7g

🕒 15 mins plus several hrs for marinating   ⏱ 15 mins

SERVES 4

I N G R E D I E N T S

2 garlic cloves, peeled

1 piece preserved ginger in syrup

1 tsp coriander seeds

2 tbsp candied ginger syrup

2 tbsp dark soy sauce

1 tbsp lime juice

1 tsp sesame oil

12 chicken wings

lime wedges and fresh cilantro leaves, to garnish

1 Roughly chop the garlic and ginger. In a pestle and mortar, crush the garlic, preserved ginger, and coriander seeds to a paste, gradually working in the ginger syrup, soy sauce, lime juice, and sesame oil.

2 Tuck the pointed tip of each chicken wing underneath the thicker end of the wing to make a neat triangular shape. Place in a large bowl.

3 Add the garlic and ginger paste to the bowl and toss the chicken wings in the mixture to coat evenly. Cover and let marinate in the refrigerator for several hours, or overnight.

4 Arrange the chicken wings in one layer on a foil-lined broiler and broil under a medium-hot broiler for 12–15 minutes, turning them occasionally, until golden brown and thoroughly cooked.

5 Alternatively, cook on a lightly oiled barbecue grill over medium-hot coals for 12–15 minutes. To serve, garnish with lime wedges and fresh cilantro.

COOK'S TIP

To test if the chicken is cooked, pierce it deeply through the thickest part of the flesh. When fully cooked, the chicken juices are clear, with no trace of pink. If there is any trace of pink, cook for a few more minutes.

Lemon Grass Skewers

An unusual recipe in which fresh lemon grass stems are used as skewers, which impart their delicate lemony flavor to the chicken mixture.

NUTRITIONAL INFORMATION

Calories 140	Sugars 2g	
Protein 19g	Fat 7g	
Carbohydrate 2g	Saturates 1g	

🄶 🄶

🍲 10 mins   🕐 20 mins

SERVES 4

I N G R E D I E N T S

2 long or 4 short lemon grass stems

2 large boneless, skinless chicken breasts (about 14 oz/400 g), roughly chopped

1 small egg white

1 carrot, finely grated

1 small red chile, deseeded and chopped

2 tbsp fresh garlic chives, chopped

2 tbsp fresh cilantro, chopped

salt and pepper

1 tbsp sunflower oil

cilantro and lime slices, to garnish

1 If the lemon grass stems are long, cut them in half across the middle to make 4 short lengths. Cut each stem in half lengthwise, so you have 8 lemon grass stems altogether.

COOK'S TIP

If you can't find whole lemon grass stems, use wooden or bamboo skewers instead, and add ¹/₂ teaspoon ground lemon grass to the mixture with the other flavorings.

2 Place the the chicken pieces in a food processor with the egg white. Process to a smooth paste, then add the carrot, chile, chives, cilantro, and salt and pepper. Process for a few seconds to mix well.

3 Chill the mixture in the refrigerator for about 15 minutes. Divide the mixture into 8 equal portions, and use your hands to shape the mixture around the lemon grass skewers.

4 Brush the skewers with oil and broil under a preheated medium-hot broiler for 4–6 minutes, turning them occasionally, until golden brown and thoroughly cooked. Alternatively, barbecue over medium-hot coals.

5 Serve hot, and garnish with slices of lime and cilantro.

Chicken Scallops

Served in scallop shells, this unusual chicken dish makes a stylish presentation for an appetizer or a light lunch.

NUTRITIONAL INFORMATION

Calories ....532 Sugars 3g
Protein ....25g Fat 34g
Carbohydrate ...33g Saturates 14g

10 mins   35 mins

SERVES 4

INGREDIENTS

6 oz/175 g short-cut macaroni, or other short pasta shapes

3 tbsp vegetable oil, plus extra for brushing

1 onion, chopped finely

3 rashers unsmoked Canadian bacon, rind removed, chopped

4¼ oz/125 g button mushrooms, sliced thinly or chopped

6 oz/175 g cooked chicken, diced

¾ cup unsweetened, plain yogurt

4 tbsp dry breadcrumbs

2¼ oz/60 g sharp Cheddar, grated

salt and pepper

flatleaf parsley sprigs, to garnish

1 Cook the pasta in a large pan of boiling salted water with 1 tablespoon of oil for 8–10 minutes. Drain the pasta, return to the pan, and cover.

2 Heat the broiler to medium. Heat the remaining oil in a pan over medium heat and fry the onion until translucent. Add the bacon and mushrooms and cook for 3–4 minutes, stirring once or twice.

3 Stir in the pasta, chicken, and plain yogurt and season to taste with salt and pepper.

4 Brush four large scallop shells with oil. Spoon in the chicken mixture and smooth to make neat mounds.

5 Mix together the breadcrumbs and cheese, and sprinkle over the top of the shells. Press the topping lightly into the chicken mixture, and broil for 4–5 minutes, until golden brown and bubbling. Garnish with sprigs of flatleaf parsley, and serve hot.

Chicken & Mango Stir-Fry

A colorful, exotic mix of flavors that works surprisingly well in a dish that is easy and quick to cook – ideal for a midweek family meal.

NUTRITIONAL INFORMATION

Calories 200   Sugars 5g
Protein ....23g   Fat 6g
Carbohydrate ....7g   Saturates 1g

15 mins   12 mins

SERVES 4

INGREDIENTS

6 boneless, skinless chicken thighs

2 tsp fresh root ginger, grated

1 garlic clove, crushed

1 small red chile, deseeded

1 large red bell pepper

4 scallions

7 oz/200 g snow peas

3½ oz/100 g baby corn cobs

1 large, firm, ripe mango

2 tbsp sunflower oil

1 tbsp light soy sauce

3 tbsp rice wine or sherry

1 tsp sesame oil

salt and pepper

snipped chives, to garnish

1 Cut the chicken into long, thin strips and place in a bowl. Mix together the ginger, garlic, and chile, then stir in to the chicken strips to coat them evenly.

2 Slice the bell pepper thinly, cutting diagonally. Trim and diagonally slice the scallions. Cut the snow peas and corn in half diagonally. Peel the mango, remove the stone, and slice thinly.

3 Heat the oil in a large skillet or wok over a high heat. Add the chicken and stir-fry for 4–5 minutes, or until just turning golden brown. Add the bell peppers and stir-fry over a medium heat for 4–5 minutes to soften them.

4 Add the scallions and snow peas together with the corn and stir-fry for another minute.

5 Mix together the soy sauce, rice wine or sherry, and sesame oil in a separate bowl and stir the mixture into the wok with the rest of the ingredients. Add the mango and stir gently for 1 minute to heat thoroughly.

6 Adjust the seasoning with salt and pepper to taste and serve immediately. Garnish with chives.

Green Chicken Curry

Thai curries are traditionally very hot, and they make a little go a long way. The spiced juices are eaten with rice to "stretch" a small amount of meat.

NUTRITIONAL INFORMATION

Calories 193	Sugars 9g	
Protein 22g	Fat 8g	
Carbohydrate 9g	Saturates 1g	

5 mins   45 mins

SERVES 4

INGREDIENTS

6 boneless, skinless chicken thighs

1¾ cups coconut milk

2 garlic cloves, crushed

2 tbsp Thai fish sauce

2 tbsp Thai green curry paste

12 baby eggplants (or Thai pea eggplants)

3 green chiles, finely chopped

3 kaffir lime leaves, shredded

4 tbsp fresh chopped cilantro

salt and pepper

boiled rice, to serve

1 Cut the chicken into bite-sized pieces. Pour the coconut milk into a large pan or wok over a high heat and bring to a boil.

2 Add the chicken, garlic, and fish sauce to the pan and bring back to a boil. Lower the heat and simmer gently for 30 minutes, or until the chicken is tender.

3 Remove the chicken from the mixture with a perforated spoon. Set aside and keep warm.

4 Stir the green curry paste into the pan, then add the eggplants, chiles, and lime leaves and simmer for 5 minutes.

5 Return the chicken to the pan and bring to a boil. Adjust the seasoning to taste with salt and pepper, then stir in the cilantro. Serve the Green Chicken Curry with boiled rice.

COOK'S TIP
Baby eggplants, or "pea eggplants" as they are called in Thailand, are traditionally used, but not always available outside the country. If you can't find them in an Oriental food store, use chopped ordinary eggplant or a few green peas.

Spicy Garlic Chicken

The intense flavors of this dish are brought out by gentle cooking. The meat should seem almost to fall off the bone and melt into the sauce.

NUTRITIONAL INFORMATION

Calories 282   Sugars 3g
Protein . . . . .29g   Fat 16g
Carbohydrate . . . .5g   Saturates 3g

10 mins   50 mins

SERVES 4

INGREDIENTS

4 garlic cloves, chopped

4 shallots, chopped

2 small red chiles, deseeded and chopped

1 lemon grass stem, finely chopped

1 tbsp fresh chopped cilantro

1 tsp shrimp paste

½ tsp ground cinnamon

1 tbsp tamarind paste

2 tbsp vegetable oil

8 small chicken joints, such as drumsticks or thighs

1¼ cups chicken bouillon

1 tbsp Thai fish sauce

1 tbsp smooth peanut butter

salt and pepper

4 tbsp toasted peanuts, chopped

stir-fried vegetables and boiled noodles, to serve

1 Place the garlic, shallots, chiles, lemon grass, cilantro, and shrimp paste in a pestle and mortar and grind to an almost smooth paste. Add the cinnamon and tamarind paste to the mixture.

2 Heat the oil in a wok or wide skillet. Add the chicken joints, turning often, until they are golden brown on all sides. Remove them from the wok and keep hot. Tip away any excess fat.

3 Add the spice paste to the wok or skillet and stir over a medium heat until lightly browned. Stir in the bouillon and return the chicken to the pan.

4 Bring to a boil, then cover tightly, lower the heat, and simmer for 25–30 minutes, stirring occasionally, until the chicken is tender and thoroughly cooked. Stir in the fish sauce and peanut butter and simmer the mixture gently for another 10 minutes.

5 Adjust the seasoning with salt and pepper to taste and scatter the toasted peanuts over the chicken. Serve hot, with colorful stir-fry vegetables and noodles.

Spanish Chicken with Garlic

Slow cooking removes any harsh flavoring from the garlic cloves and makes them perfectly tender in this simple dish.

NUTRITIONAL INFORMATION

Calories 496   Sugars 1g
Protein ....41g   Fat 22g
Carbohydrate ...15g   Saturates 5g

10 mins   50 mins

SERVES 4

INGREDIENTS

2–3 tbsp all-purpose flour

cayenne pepper

4 chicken quarters or other joints, patted dry

4–5 tbsp olive oil

20 large garlic cloves, halved and green cores removed

1 large bay leaf

2 cups chicken bouillon

4 tbsp dry white wine

salt and pepper

fresh chopped parsley, to garnish

1 Put 2 tablespoons of the flour in a plastic bag and season to taste with cayenne pepper and salt and pepper. Add each chicken piece to the bag and shake until lightly coated, then shake off the excess.

2 Heat 3 tablespoons of the olive oil in a large skillet. Add the garlic cloves and fry for about 2 minutes. Remove with a slotted spoon and set aside.

3 Add the chicken pieces to the pan, skin-side down, and fry for 5 minutes, or until the skin is golden brown. Turn and fry for another 5 minutes, adding an extra 1–2 tablespoons oil if necessary.

4 Return the garlic to the pan. Add the bay leaf, bouillon, and wine and bring to a boil. Lower the heat, cover, then simmer for 25 minutes, or until the chicken is tender.

5 Using a slotted spoon, transfer the chicken to a serving platter and keep warm. Bring the cooking liquid to a boil, with the garlic, and boil until reduced to about 1 cup. Adjust the seasoning, if necessary.

6 Spoon the sauce over the chicken pieces and scatter the garlic cloves. Garnish with parsley and serve.

COOK'S TIP

The cooked garlic cloves are delicious mashed into a paste on the side of the plate for smearing on the chicken pieces.

Chicken Basquaise

Bell peppers an ingredient often used in the Basque cooking of France, are combined in this dish with the traditional air-dried ham of Bayonne.

NUTRITIONAL INFORMATION

Calories	559	Sugars	.........8g
Protein	........50g	Fat	..........21g
Carbohydrate	...44g	Saturates	.......6g

20 mins   1 hr 30 mins

SERVES 4–5

INGREDIENTS

3 lb/1.3 kg chicken, cut into 8 pieces

flour, for dusting

2–3 tbsp olive oil

1 large onion (preferably Spanish), thickly sliced

2 bell peppers, deseeded and cut lengthwise into thick strips

2 garlic cloves

5½ oz/150 g spicy chorizo sausage, peeled, if necessary, and cut into ½ inch/1 cm pieces

1 tbsp tomato paste

1 cup long-grain white rice or medium-grain Spanish rice, such as Valencia

2 cups chicken bouillon

1 tsp crushed dried chilis

½ tsp dried thyme

4¼ oz/120 g Bayonne or other air-dried ham, diced

12 dry-cured black olives

2 tbsp chopped fresh flatleaf parsley

salt and pepper

1 Dry the chicken pieces well with paper towels. Put about 2 tablespoons flour into a plastic bag, season with salt and pepper and add the chicken pieces. Seal the bag and shake to coat the chicken.

2 Heat 2 tablespoons of the oil in a large casserole. Add the chicken and cook for 15 minutes. Transfer to a plate.

3 Heat the remaining oil in the casserole and add the onion and peppers. Reduce the heat and stir-fry briefly. Add the garlic, chorizo, and tomato paste and stir for about 3 minutes. Add the rice and cook for about 2 minutes, stirring to coat.

4 Add the bouillon, crushed chilis, and thyme and seasoning. Bring to a boil. Return the chicken to the pan, cover, and cook over a low heat for about 45 minutes.

5 Gently stir the ham, black olives, and half the parsley into the rice mixture. Re-cover and heat through for another 5 minutes. Sprinkle with the remaining parsley, and serve.

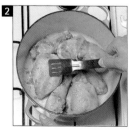

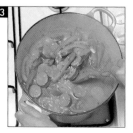

Chicken in Green Salsa

Chicken breasts bathed in a fragrant sauce make a delicate dish, perfect for dinner parties. Serve with rice to complete the meal.

NUTRITIONAL INFORMATION

Calories	349	Sugars	.........7g
Protein	........34g	Fat	..........20g
Carbohydrate	...10g	Saturates	......12g

10 mins

35 mins

SERVES 4

I N G R E D I E N T S

4 chicken breast fillets

flour, for dredging

2–3 tbsp butter or combination of butter and oil

1 lb/450 g mild green salsa or puréed tomatillos

1 cup chicken bouillon

1–2 garlic cloves, finely chopped

3–5 tbsp fresh chopped cilantro

½ fresh green chile, deseeded and chopped

½ tsp ground cumin

salt and pepper

TO SERVE

1 cup sour cream

several leaves romaine lettuce, shredded

3–5 scallions, thinly sliced

fresh cilantro, coarsely-chopped

1 Sprinkle the chicken with salt and pepper, then dredge in flour. Shake off the excess flour.

2 Melt the butter in a skillet, then add the chicken, and cook over a medium-high heat, turning once, until they are golden but not cooked through – they will continue to cook slightly in the sauce. Remove from the skillet and set aside.

3 Place the salsa, chicken bouillon, garlic, cilantro, chile, and cumin in a pan and bring to a boil. Reduce the heat to a low simmer. Add the chicken breasts to the sauce, spooning the sauce over the chicken. Continue to cook for up to 15 minutes, or until the chicken is cooked through.

4 Remove the chicken breasts from the pan and season with salt and pepper to taste. Serve with the sour cream, the shredded lettuce leaves, the sliced scallions, and the chopped fresh chopped cilantro leaves.

Citrus-Marinated Chicken

This is a great dish for a summer meal. The marinade gives the chicken an appetizing flavor and helps keeps it succulent and moist during cooking.

NUTRITIONAL INFORMATION

Calories 315	Sugars 2g	
Protein 42g	Fat 41g	
Carbohydrate 4g	Saturates 6g	

10 mins, plus at least 1 hr to marinate

25 mins

SERVES 4

INGREDIENTS

1 chicken, cut into 4 pieces

1 tbsp mild chili powder

1 tbsp paprika

2 tsp ground cumin

1 orange, juice and zest

3 limes, juiced

pinch of sugar

8–10 garlic cloves, finely chopped

1 bunch fresh cilantro, coarsely chopped

2–3 tbsp extra-virgin olive oil

¼ cup beer, tequila, or pineapple juice, optional

salt and pepper

TO SERVE

lime wedges

tomato, pepper, and scallion salad

fresh cilantro sprigs

1 Place the chicken in a non-metallic dish. To make the marinade, mix the remaining ingredients in a bowl and season.

2 Pour the marinade over the chicken, turn to coat well, then let marinate for at least an hour at room temperature. If possible, leave for 24 hours in the refrigerator to marinate.

3 Remove the chicken from the marinade and pat dry thoroughly with paper towels.

4 Put the chicken on a broiler pan and place under a preheated broiler for 20–25 minutes, turning once, until the chicken is cooked through. Alternatively, cook in a ridged pan. Brush with the marinade occasionally. Pierce a thick part with a skewer—the juices should run clear.

5 Garnish with cilantro and serve the chicken with lime wedges and a refreshing side salad.

Squabs in Green Marinade

Marinated before cooking in a green herb mixture, these elegant squabs are packed with lively Mexican flavors.

NUTRITIONAL INFORMATION

Calories	614	Sugars	.........6g
Protein	........44g	Fat	..........49g
Carbohydrate	....8g	Saturates	......19g

10 mins plus at least 3 hrs to marinate

45 mins

SERVES 4

INGREDIENTS

10 garlic cloves, chopped

1 lime, juiced

1 bunch fresh cilantro, finely chopped

½ fresh green chile, deseeded and chopped

1 tsp ground cumin

4 squabs

12 oz/350 g plain, unsweetened yogurt

1 red bell pepper, roasted, peeled, deseeded, and diced

¼–1 tsp marinade from chipotle canned in adobo, or chipotle salsa

3–5 scallions, thinly sliced

handful of toasted pumpkin seeds

salt and pepper

1 Combine 9 garlic cloves with the lime juice, three-quarters of the cilantro, green chile, and half the cumin in a bowl. Press the mixture on to the squabs and marinate for at least 3 hours in the refrigerator, or preferably overnight.

2 Place the squabs in a roasting pan and cook in a preheated oven at 400°F/200°C for 15 minutes. To check whether it is cooked, pierce the thigh with a knife. If the juices run clear, the squab is cooked; if necessary, return to the oven and continue to roast.

3 Meanwhile, mix the plain yogurt with the pepper, chipotle marinade, and the remaining garlic and cumin. Season with salt and pepper to taste.

4 Serve each squab individually with a spoonful of the pepper sauce and a sprinkling of the remaining fresh cilantro, the scallions, and the pumpkin seeds. Serve the dish right away while the chicken is still piping hot.

VARIATION

For barbecued lamb, skewer lamb chunks, such as shoulder or leg, on to metal or soaked bamboo skewers. Marinate in the green herbed marinade as in Step 1, then cook over the hot coals of a barbecue.

Chicken & Potato Casserole

Small new potatoes are ideal for this recipe because they can be cooked whole. Cut larger potatoes in half or into chunks before using them.

NUTRITIONAL INFORMATION

Calories	856	Sugars	.........7g
Protein	........35g	Fat	..........58g
Carbohydrate	...40g	Saturates	......26g

15 mins   1 hr 35 mins

SERVES 4

INGREDIENTS

2 tbsp vegetable oil

4 chicken portions (about 8 oz/225 g each)

2 leeks, sliced

1 garlic clove, crushed

4 tbsp all-purpose flour

3½ cups chicken bouillon

1¼ cups dry white wine

4¼ oz/125 g baby carrots, halved lengthwise

4¼ oz/125 g baby corn cobs, halved lengthwise

1 lb/450 g small new potatoes

1 bouquet garni sachet

⅔ cup heavy cream

salt and pepper

1 Heat the oil in a large skillet. Cook the chicken for 10 minutes, turning until browned. Transfer the chicken to a casserole dish using a perforated spoon.

2 Add the leek and garlic and cook for 2–3 minutes, stirring. Stir in the flour, cook for 1 minute and remove from the heat. Stir in the bouillon and wine.

3 Return the skillet to the heat and bring to a boil. Stir in the carrots, corn, the potatoes, and bouquet garni, and season. to taste. Transfer to the casserole dish.

4 Cover and cook in a preheated oven, 350°F/180°C, for 1 hour.

5 Remove the casserole to stir in the cream. Return to the oven, uncovered, and cook for 15 minutes. Remove the bouquet garni, season and serve with rice.

COOK'S TIP

Use turkey fillets instead of the chicken, if preferred, and vary the vegetables according to those you have to hand.

Potato, Leek, & Chicken Pie

This pie has an attractive phyllo pastry case with a ruffled top made from strips of the pastry brushed with melted butter.

NUTRITIONAL INFORMATION

Calories	543	Sugars	.........7g
Protein	........21g	Fat	..........27g
Carbohydrate	...56g	Saturates	......16g

15 mins   1 hr 5 mins

SERVES 4

I N G R E D I E N T S

8 oz/225 g waxy potatoes, cubed

5 tbsp butter

1 skinned chicken breast fillet (about 6 oz/175 g), cubed

1 leek, sliced

5½ oz/150 g chestnut mushrooms, sliced

2½ tbsp all-purpose flour

1¼ cups milk

1 tbsp Dijon mustard

2 tbsp chopped fresh sage

8 oz/225 g phyllo pastry, thawed if frozen

3 tbsp butter, melted

salt and pepper

1 Cook the cubed potato in a saucepan of boiling water for 5 minutes; drain.

2 Melt the butter in a skillet and cook the chicken cubes for 5 minutes.

3 Add the leek and mushrooms, and cook for 3 minutes, stirring. Stir in the flour and cook for 1 minute. Gradually add the milk and bring to a boil. Add the mustard, sage, and potatoes, season, then let the mixture simmer for 10 minutes.

4 Meanwhile, line a deep pie dish with half the sheets of phyllo pastry. Spoon the sauce into the dish and cover with one sheet of pastry. Brush the pastry with butter and lay another sheet on top. Brush this sheet with more butter.

5 Cut the remaining phyllo pastry into strips and fold them on top of the pie creating a ruffled effect. Brush the strips with the melted butter and cook in a preheated oven, 350°F/180°C, for 45 minutes, or until golden brown and crisp. Serve hot.

COOK'S TIP

If the top of the pie starts to brown too quickly, cover it with foil halfway through the cooking time to let the pastry base cook through without the top burning.

Chicken Suprêmes Nellwyn

The refreshing combination of chicken and orange sauce with whole-wheat spaghetti makes this a perfect dish for a warm summer evening.

NUTRITIONAL INFORMATION

Calories	933	Sugars	........34g
Protein	........74g	Fat	..........24g
Carbohydrate	..100g	Saturates	.......5g

10 mins   35 mins

SERVES 4

INGREDIENTS

2 tbsp rapeseed oil

3 tbsp olive oil

4 x 8 oz/225 g chicken suprêmes

⅔ cup orange brandy

2 tbsp all-purpose flour

⅔ cup freshly-squeezed
   orange juice

1 oz/25 g zucchini, cut into matchstick
   strips

1 oz/25 g red bell pepper, cut into
   matchstick strips

1 oz/25 g leek, finely shredded

salt and pepper

14 oz/400 g dried whole-wheat spaghetti

3 large oranges, peeled and cut
   into segments

1 orange, zest cut into very fine strips

2 tbsp chopped fresh tarragon

⅔ cup ricotta cheese

fresh tarragon leaves, to garnish

1 Heat the rapeseed oil and 1 tbsp of the olive oil in a skillet. Add the chicken and cook quickly until golden brown. Add the orange brandy and cook for 3 minutes. Sprinkle over the flour and cook for 2 minutes.

2 Lower the heat and add the orange juice, zucchini, pepper, and leek and season to taste. Simmer for 5 minutes, or until the sauce has thickened.

3 Meanwhile, bring a pan of salted water to a boil. Add the spaghetti and 1 tbsp of the olive oil and cook for 10 minutes. Drain, then transfer to a serving dish and drizzle over the remaining oil.

4 Add half the orange segments, half the orange zest, the tarragon, and ricotta cheese to the sauce in the pan and cook for 3 minutes.

5 Place the chicken on top of the spaghetti, pour over a little sauce, garnish with the remaining orange segments, zest, and tarragon. Serve immediately.

Chicken & Lobster on Penne

This dish provides a touch of luxury for the tastebuds, yet it is not extravagant because it uses just a small amount of lobster.

NUTRITIONAL INFORMATION

Calories ....696 Sugars 4g
Protein ....59g Fat 32g
Carbohydrate ...45g Saturates 9g

10 mins   45 mins

SERVES 6

INGREDIENTS

butter, for greasing

6 chicken breasts

1 lb/450 g dried penne rigati

6 tbsp extra virgin olive oil

¾ cup freshly grated
   Parmesan cheese

FILLING

4 oz/115 g lobster meat, chopped

2 shallots, very finely chopped

2 figs, chopped

1 tbsp garam marsala

2 tbsp bread crumbs

1 large egg, beaten

salt and pepper

1 Grease 6 pieces of kitchen foil, which are large enough to enclose the chicken breasts, and lightly grease a cookie sheet.

2 Place all of the filling ingredients into a mixing bowl and blend together thoroughly with a spoon.

3 Cut a pocket in each chicken breast with a sharp knife and fill with the lobster mixture. Wrap the chicken in the foil, place the parcels on the greased cookie sheet and bake in a preheated oven at 400°F/200°C for 30 minutes.

4 Meanwhile, bring a large pan of lightly salted water to a boil. Add the pasta and 1 tbsp of the olive oil and cook for about 10 minutes, or until tender but still firm to the bite. Drain the pasta thoroughly and transfer to a large serving plate. Sprinkle over the remaining olive oil and the grated Parmesan cheese, then set aside and keep warm.

5 Carefully remove the foil from around the chicken breasts. Slice the breasts very thinly, then arrange over the pasta and serve immediately.

COOK'S TIP

The cut of chicken known as suprême consists of the breast and wing. It is always skinned.

Pan-Cooked Chicken

Artichokes are a familiar ingredient in traditional Italian cooking. In this dish, they are used to delicately flavor chicken breasts.

NUTRITIONAL INFORMATION

Calories 296   Sugars 2g
Protein ....27g   Fat 15g
Carbohydrate ....7g   Saturates 6g

15 mins   55 mins

SERVES 4

INGREDIENTS

4 chicken breasts, part-boned

salt and pepper

2 tbsp olive oil

2 tbsp butter

2 red onions, cut into wedges

2 tbsp lemon juice

⅔ cup dry white wine

⅔ cup chicken bouillon

2 tsp all-purpose flour

14 oz/400 g can artichoke halves, drained and halved

chopped fresh parsley, to garnish

1 Season the chicken with salt and pepper according to taste. Heat the oil and 1 tablespoon of the butter in a large skillet. Add the chicken and fry for 4–5 minutes on each side, or until lightly golden. Remove from the pan using a slotted spoon.

2 Toss the onion in the lemon juice, and add to the skillet. Gently fry, stirring, for 3–4 minutes, or until the onion is just beginning to soften.

3 Return the partly cooked chicken to the skillet. Pour in the wine and bouillon, then bring to a boil. Cover and simmer gently for 30 minutes.

4 Remove the chicken from the skillet. Carefully reserve the cooking juices, and keep them warm to one side. Bring the juices to a boil, and boil rapidly for 5 minutes.

5 Blend the remaining butter with the flour to form a paste. Reduce the reserved warm juices to a simmer and spoon the paste into the skillet, stirring until thickened.

6 Adjust the seasoning according to taste, stir in the artichoke hearts, then cook for another 2 minutes. Pour the mixture over the chicken and garnish with chopped parsley.

Italian Chicken Parcels

This cooking method makes the chicken aromatic and succulent, and because the ingredients cook in their own juices it uses a minimum of oil.

NUTRITIONAL INFORMATION

Calories	234	Sugars	.........5g
Protein	........28g	Fat	..........12g
Carbohydrate	....5g	Saturates	.......5g

20 mins   30 mins

SERVES 6

INGREDIENTS

1 tbsp olive oil

6 skinless chicken breast fillets

9 oz/250 g Mozzarella cheese

1 lb 2 oz/500 g zucchinis, sliced

6 large tomatoes, sliced

1 small bunch fresh basil or oregano

pepper

rice or pasta, to serve

1 Cut 6 pieces of kitchen foil, each piece measuring approximately 10 inches/25 cm square. Brush the foil squares lightly with olive oil and set aside until required.

2 With a sharp knife, slash each chicken breast at regular intervals. Slice the Mozzarella cheese and place between the cuts in the chicken.

3 Divide the zucchinis and tomatoes between the pieces of foil, then sprinkle with pepper to taste. Tear or roughly chop the basil or oregano and scatter over the vegetables in each parcel.

4 Place the chicken on top of each pile of vegetables, then season with pepper. Wrap in the foil to enclose the chicken and vegetables, tucking in the ends.

5 Place on a baking tray and bake in a preheated oven, 400°C/200°C, for about 30 minutes.

6 To serve, unwrap each foil parcel and serve with rice or pasta.

COOK'S TIP

To aid cooking, place the vegetables and chicken on the shiny side of the foil. This ensures that the heat is absorbed into the parcel and not reflected away from it.

Prosciutto-Wrapped Chicken

Stuffed with ricotta, nutmeg, and spinach, and wrapped in wafer-thin slices of prosciutto, this chicken is then gently cooked in white wine.

NUTRITIONAL INFORMATION

Calories 426   Sugars 4g
Protein . . . . .44g   Fat 21g
Carbohydrate . . . .9g   Saturates 8g

20 mins   40 mins

SERVES 4

INGREDIENTS

4¼ oz/125 g frozen spinach, defrosted

4¼ oz/125 g ricotta cheese

pinch of grated nutmeg

salt and pepper

4 skinless, boneless chicken breasts (each weighing about 6 oz/175 g)

4 prosciutto slices

2 tbsp butter

1 tbsp olive oil

12 small onions or shallots

4½ oz/125 g button mushrooms, sliced

1 tbsp all-purpose flour

⅔ cup dry white or red wine

1¼ cups chicken bouillon

1 Put the spinach into a strainer and press out the water with a spoon. Mix with the ricotta and nutmeg, then season with salt and pepper to taste.

2 Using a sharp knife, slit each chicken breast through the side and enlarge each cut to form a pocket. Fill each cut with the spinach mixture, then reshape the chicken breasts to enclose the mixture. Wrap each breast tightly in a slice of ham, and secure with toothpicks. Cover and chill in the refrigerator.

3 Heat the butter and oil in a skillet and brown the chicken breasts for at least 2 minutes on each side. Transfer the chicken to a large, shallow ovenproof dish and keep warm until required.

4 Fry the onions and mushrooms for 2–3 minutes, or until lightly browned. Stir in the all-purpose flour, then gradually add the wine and bouillon.

Bring to a boil, stirring constantly. Season with salt and pepper to taste, and spoon the mixture around the chicken.

5 Cook the chicken uncovered in a preheated oven, 400°F/200°C, for 20 minutes. Turn the breasts over and cook for another 10 minutes. Remove the toothpicks and serve with the sauce, together with carrot paste and green beans, if desired.

Chicken Risotto Milanese

This simple chicken risotto is one of Italy's best-known dishes, served in restaurants all over the world. But every cook varies the recipe slightly.

NUTRITIONAL INFORMATION

Calories ....857 Sugars 1g
Protein ....57g Fat 38g
Carbohydrate ...72g Saturates 21g

5 mins   1 hr 5 mins

SERVES 4

I N G R E D I E N T S

4¼ oz/125 g/butter

2 lb/900 g chicken, sliced thinly

1 large onion, chopped

1 lb 2 oz/500 g risotto rice

2½ cups chicken bouillon

⅔ cup white wine

1 tsp crumbled saffron

salt and pepper

generous ½ cup grated Parmesan cheese, to serve

1 Heat 4 tbsp of butter in a deep skillet, and fry the chicken and onion until golden brown.

2 Add the rice to the skillet, stir well, then cook for 15 minutes.

3 Heat the bouillon until boiling and gradually add to the rice. Add the white wine, saffron, salt and pepper, and mix well. Simmer gently for 20 minutes, stirring occasionally, and adding more bouillon if the risotto becomes too dry.

4 Let the risotto stand for 2–3 minutes and just before serving, add a little more bouillon and simmer for 10 minutes. Serve the risotto, sprinkled with the grated Parmesan cheese and the remaining butter.

Kung Po Chicken

Cashew nuts are a principal ingredient in this traditional Szechuan recipe, but peanuts, walnuts, or almonds may be used instead.

NUTRITIONAL INFORMATION

Calories	294	Sugars	.........3g
Protein	........21g	Fat	..........18g
Carbohydrate	...10g	Saturates	.......4g

10 mins   10 mins

SERVES 4

INGREDIENTS

9–10½ oz/250–300 g chicken, boned and skinned

¼ tsp salt

⅓ egg white

1 tsp cornstarch paste (see page 39)

1 green bell pepper, cored and seeded

4 tbsp vegetable oil

1 scallion, cut into short sections

½ inch/1cm fresh root ginger, sliced

4–5 small dried red chilis, soaked, deseeded, and shredded

2 tbsp crushed yellow bean sauce

1 tsp rice wine or dry sherry

4¼ oz/125 g roasted cashew nuts

drops of sesame oil

boiled rice, to serve

1 Cut the chicken into small cubes about the size of sugar lumps. Place the chicken in a small bowl and mix with a pinch of salt, the egg white, and the cornstarch paste, in that order.

2 Cut the green bell pepper into cubes or triangles about the same size as the chicken pieces.

3 Heat the oil in a wok, add the chicken, then stir-fry for 1 minute. Remove the chicken with a slotted spoon and keep warm.

4 Add the scallion, ginger, chilis, and green bell pepper. Stir-fry for 1 minute, then add the chicken with the yellow bean sauce, and wine. Blend well and stir-fry for another minute. Finally stir in the cashew nuts and sesame oil. Serve hot with boiled rice.

VARIATION

Any nuts can be used in place of the cashew nuts, if preferred. The important point is the crunchy texture, which is very much a feature of Szechuan cooking.

Lemon Chicken

This is on everyone's list of favorite Chinese dishes, perhaps because it is so simple to make. Serve with stir-fried vegetables for a delicious meal.

NUTRITIONAL INFORMATION

Calories 272	Sugars 1g
Protein 36g	Fat 11g
Carbohydrate 5g	Saturates 2g

5 mins   15 mins

SERVES 4

INGREDIENTS

vegetable oil, for deep-frying

1 lb 7 oz/650 g skinless, boneless chicken, cut into strips

SAUCE

1 tbsp cornstarch

6 tbsp cold water

3 tbsp fresh lemon juice

2 tbsp sweet sherry

½ tsp superfine sugar

GARNISH

lemon slices

shredded scallion

1 Heat the oil for deep-frying in a wok or skillet to 350°F/180°C, or until a bread cube browns in 30 seconds.

2 Reduce the heat and stir-fry the chicken strips for 3–4 minutes, or until cooked through.

3 Remove the chicken with a slotted spoon, set aside and keep warm. Drain the oil from the wok.

4 To make the sauce, mix the cornstarch with 2 tablespoons of the water to form a paste.

5 Pour the lemon juice and remaining water into the mixture in the wok.

6 Add the sherry and superfine sugar and bring to a boil, stirring until the sugar has completely dissolved.

7 Stir in the cornstarch sauce and return to a boil. Reduce the heat and simmer, stirring constantly, for 2–3 minutes, or until the sauce is thickened and clear.

8 Transfer the chicken to a warm serving plate and pour the sauce over the top. Garnish with the lemon slices and shredded scallion and serve immediately.

COOK'S TIP

If you would prefer to use chicken portions rather than strips, cook them in the oil, covered, over a low heat for about 30 minutes, or until cooked through.

Peanut Sesame Chicken

Sesame seeds and peanuts give extra crunch and flavor to this stir-fry, and the fruit juice glaze gives the sauce a glossy coating.

NUTRITIONAL INFORMATION

Calories ....435 Sugars 10g
Protein ....38g Fat 26g
Carbohydrate ...14g Saturates 4g

10 mins   15 mins

SERVES 4

INGREDIENTS

2 tbsp vegetable oil

2 tbsp sesame oil

1 lb 2 oz/500 g boneless, skinned chicken
    breasts, sliced into strips

9 oz/250 g broccoli, divided into small florets

9 oz/250 g baby or dwarf corn,
    halved if large

1 small red bell pepper, cored,
    deseeded, and sliced

2 tbsp soy sauce

1 cup orange juice

2 tsp cornstarch

2 tbsp sesame seeds, toasted

2¼ oz/60 g roasted, shelled,
    unsalted peanuts

rice or noodles, to serve

COOK'S TIP

Make sure you use the unsalted
variety of peanuts or the dish will
be too salty, as the soy sauce adds
extra saltiness.

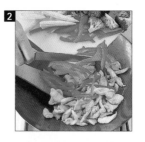

1 Heat the oils in a large, heavy-based skillet or wok until smoking. Add the chicken strips and stir-fry for about 4–5 minutes, or until browned.

2 Add the broccoli, corn, and red bell pepper, and stir-fry over a high heat for 1–2 minutes, until they just soften.

3 Meanwhile, mix the soy sauce together with the orange juice and the cornstarch. Stir into the chicken and vegetable mixture, stirring constantly until the sauce has slightly thickened and a glaze develops.

4 Stir in the sesame seeds and peanuts, mixing well. Heat the stir-fry for another 3–4 minutes.

5 Transfer the stir-fry to a warm serving dish and serve with rice or noodles.

Braised Chicken

A glaze served with the chicken a sauce gives this straightforward whole chicken dish a professional touch.

NUTRITIONAL INFORMATION

Calories ....294 Sugars 9g
Protein ....31g Fat 15g
Carbohydrate ...10g Saturates 3g

10 mins   1 hr 15 mins

SERVES 4

INGREDIENTS

3 lb 5 oz/1.5 kg chicken

3 tbsp vegetable oil

1 tbsp peanut oil

2 tbsp dark brown sugar

5 tbsp dark soy sauce

⅔ cup water

2 garlic cloves, crushed

1 small onion, chopped

1 fresh red chile, chopped

celery leaves and chives, to garnish

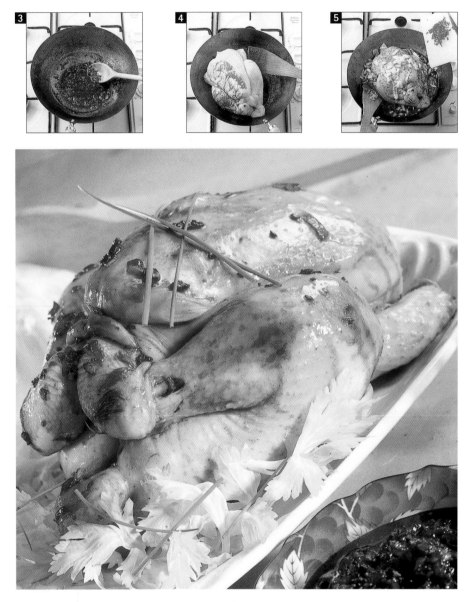

1 Preheat a large wok or large skillet in preparation.

2 Clean the chicken inside and out with damp paper towels.

3 Place the vegetable oil and peanut oil in the wok, then add the dark brown sugar and heat together gently until the sugar caramelizes.

4 Stir the soy sauce into the wok. Add the chicken and turn it in the mixture to coat thoroughly on all sides.

5 Add the water, crushed garlic, chopped onion, and chopped chile. Cover and simmer, turning the chicken occasionally, for about 1 hour, or until cooked through.

6 Remove the chicken from the wok and set it to one side. Increase the heat and reduce the sauce in the wok until it has thickened. Transfer the chicken to a serving plate. Garnish with celery leaves and chives, and serve with the sauce.

COOK'S TIP

For a spicier sauce, add 1 tbsp of finely chopped fresh ginger and 1 tbsp ground Szechuan peppercorns with the chile in Step 5.

Chicken & Rice Casserole

This is a quick-cooking, spicy casserole of rice, chicken, and vegetables in an aromatic soy and ginger-flavored liquor.

NUTRITIONAL INFORMATION

Calories 502	Sugars 2g
Protein 55g	Fat 9g
Carbohydrate ...52g	Saturates 3g

15 mins, plus 30 mins to marinate

45 mins

SERVES 4

INGREDIENTS

⅔ cup long-grain rice

1 tbsp dry sherry

2 tbsp light soy sauce

2 tbsp dark soy sauce

2 tsp dark brown sugar

1 tsp salt

1 tsp sesame oil

900 g/2 lb skinless, boneless chicken meat, diced

3¾ cups chicken bouillon

2 open-cup mushrooms, sliced

60 g/2¼ oz water chestnuts, halved

75 g/2¾ oz broccoli florets

1 yellow (bell) pepper, sliced

4 tsp grated fresh root ginger

whole chives, to garnish

1 Cook the rice in boiling water for 15 minutes. Drain well, rinse under cold water, then drain again thoroughly.

2 Mix together the sherry, soy sauces, sugar, salt, and sesame oil.

3 Stir the chicken into the soy mixture, turning to coat the chicken well. Let marinate for about 30 minutes.

4 Bring the bouillon to a boil in a saucepan or wok. Add the chicken with the marinade, mushrooms, water chestnuts, broccoli, pepper, and ginger.

5 Stir in the rice, reduce the heat, then cover and cook for 25-30 minutes, or until the chicken and vegetables are cooked through. Transfer to serving plates, garnish with chives and serve.

VARIATION

This dish would work equally well with beef or pork. Chinese dried mushrooms may be used instead of the open-cup mushrooms, if rehydrated before adding to the dish.

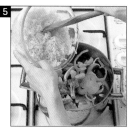

Sage Chicken & Rice

Cooking in a single pot means that all of the flavors are retained. This is a substantial meal that needs only a salad and some crusty bread.

NUTRITIONAL INFORMATION

Calories 247	Sugars 5g	
Protein 26g	Fat 5g	
Carbohydrate ...25g	Saturates 2g	

🕐 15 mins   ⏱ 45 mins

SERVES 4

INGREDIENTS

1 large onion, chopped

1 garlic clove, crushed

2 celery stalks, sliced

2 carrots, diced

2 sprigs fresh sage

1¼ cups chicken bouillon

12 oz/350 g boneless, skinless
   chicken breasts

generous 1 cup mixed brown and wild rice

14 oz/400 g can chopped tomatoes

dash of Tabasco sauce

2 zucchinis, trimmed and thinly sliced

3½ oz/100 g lean ham, diced

salt and pepper

fresh sage, to garnish

TO SERVE

salad leaves

crusty bread

1 Place the pieces of onion, garlic, celery, carrots, and sprigs of fresh sage in a large saucepan and pour in the chicken bouillon.

2 Bring the vegetable and herb mixture to a boil, then cover the pan and let simmer for 5 minutes.

3 Cut the chicken into 1 inch/2.5 cm cubes and stir into the pan with the vegetables. Cover the pan and continue to cook for another 5 minutes.

4 Stir in the mixed brown and wild rice and chopped tomatoes.

5 Add a dash of Tabasco sauce to taste and season well. Bring to a boil, then cover and simmer for 25 minutes.

6 Carefully stir in the sliced zucchinis and diced ham and continue to cook, uncovered, for another 10 minutes, stirring occasionally, until the rice is just tender.

7 Remove the sprigs of sage and then discard them.

8 Garnish with sage leaves and serve with a salad and fresh crusty bread.

Chile Chicken Meatballs

These tender chicken and corn nuggets are served with a sweet and sour sauce. They make treats to nibble with drinks.

NUTRITIONAL INFORMATION

Calories 196   Sugars 12g
Protein ....26g   Fat 4g
Carbohydrate ...15g   Saturates 1g

30 mins   25 mins

SERVES 4

INGREDIENTS

1 lb/450 g lean chicken, ground

4 scallions, trimmed and finely chopped, plus extra to garnish

1 small red chile, deseeded and finely chopped

1 inch/2.5 cm piece fresh ginger, finely chopped

3½ oz/100 g can corn (no added sugar or salt), drained

salt and white pepper

boiled jasmine rice, to serve

SAUCE

⅔ cup fresh chicken bouillon (see page 5)

3½ oz/100 g cubed pineapple in natural juice, drained, with 4 tbsp reserved juice

1 carrot, cut into thin strips

1 small red bell pepper, deseeded and diced, plus extra to garnish

1 small green bell pepper, deseeded and diced

1 tbsp light soy sauce

2 tbsp rice vinegar

1 tbsp caster sugar

1 tbsp tomato paste

2 tsp cornstarch mixed to a paste with 4 tsp cold water

1 To make the meatballs, place the chicken in a mixing bowl and mix with the scallions, chile, ginger, corn, and salt and pepper.

2 Divide into 16 portions and form each into a ball. Bring a saucepan of water to a boil. Arrange the meatballs on baking parchment in a steamer or large strainer, place over the water, then cover and steam for 10–12 minutes.

3 To make the sauce, pour the bouillon and pineapple juice into a pan and bring to a boil. Add the carrot and peppers, then cover and simmer for 5 minutes. Add the remaining ingredients, stirring until thickened. Season and set aside.

4 Drain the meatballs and transfer to a serving plate. Garnish with snipped chives and serve with boiled rice and the sauce (reheated if necessary).

Crispy Stuffed Chicken

An attractive main course of chicken breasts filled with mixed bell peppers and set on a sea of red bell peppers and rich tomato sauce.

NUTRITIONAL INFORMATION

Calories ....196 Sugars 4g
Protein ....29g Fat 6g
Carbohydrate ....6g Saturates 2g

20 mins   50 mins

SERVES 4

INGREDIENTS

4 boneless chicken breasts, skinned
    (about 5½ oz/150 g each)

salt and pepper

4 sprigs fresh tarragon

½ small orange bell pepper, deseeded
    and sliced

½ small green bell pepper, deseeded
    and sliced

½ oz/15 g whole-wheat bread crumbs

1 tbsp sesame seeds

4 tbsp lemon juice

1 small red bell pepper, halved
    and deseeded

7 oz/200 g can chopped tomatoes

1 small red chile, deseeded and chopped

¼ tsp celery salt

fresh tarragon, to garnish

1 Preheat the oven to 400°F/200°C. Make a slit in the chicken breasts with a small, sharp knife to create a pocket in each. Season inside each pocket.

2 Place a sprig of tarragon and a few slices of the orange and green bell peppers in each chicken pocket. Place the chicken breasts on a nonstick cookie sheet and sprinkle over the bread crumbs and sesame seeds.

3 Spoon 1 tablespoon lemon juice over each chicken breast and bake in the oven for 35–40 minutes, or until the chicken is tender and cooked through.

4 Meanwhile, preheat the broiler to a hot setting. Arrange the red pepper halves, skin side up, on the broiler rack and cook for 5–6 minutes, or until the skin blisters. Let cool for 10 minutes, then peel off the skins.

5 Put the red pepper in a blender, add the tomatoes, chile, and celery salt and process for a few seconds. Season to taste. Alternatively, chop the red pepper finely and press through a strainer with the tomatoes and chile.

6 When the chicken is cooked, heat the sauce, spoon a little on to a warm plate and arrange a chicken breast in the center. Garnish with tarragon and serve.

Chicken with a Yogurt Crust

A spicy, Indian-style coating is baked around lean chicken to give a full flavor. Serve with a tomato, cucumber, and cilantro relish.

NUTRITIONAL INFORMATION

Calories 176	Sugars 5g
Protein 30g	Fat 4g
Carbohydrate 5g	Saturates 1g

10 mins   35 mins

SERVES 4

INGREDIENTS

1 garlic clove, crushed

1 inch/2.5 cm piece fresh ginger, finely chopped

1 fresh green chile, deseeded and finely chopped

6 tbsp low-fat unsweetened yogurt

1 tbsp tomato paste

1 tsp ground turmeric

1 tsp garam marsala

1 tbsp lime juice

4 boneless, skinless chicken breasts (each 4¼ oz/125 g)

salt and pepper

wedges of lime or lemon, to serve

RELISH

4 tomatoes

¼ cucumber

1 small red onion

2 tbsp fresh, chopped cilantro

1 Preheat the oven to 375°F/190°C and have ready a mixing bowl and a cookie sheet.

2 Place the garlic, ginger, chile, yogurt, tomato paste, spices, lime juice, and seasoning in a bowl and mix to combine all the ingredients.

3 Wash and pat dry the chicken breasts thoroughly with absorbent paper towels and place them on the cookie sheet.

4 Brush or spread the spicy yogurt mix over the chicken and bake in the oven for 30–35 minutes, or until the meat is tender and cooked through.

5 Meanwhile, make the relish. Finely chop the tomatoes, cucumber, and onion and mix together with the cilantro. Season with salt and pepper to taste, then cover and chill in the refrigerator until required.

6 Drain the cooked chicken on absorbent paper towels and serve hot with the relish and lemon or lime wedges. Alternatively, let cool, then chill for at least 1 hour and serve sliced as part of a salad.

Lemon & Honey Chicken

A good dish for the barbecue, this sweet and citrus-scented chicken can be served hot or cold. Sesame-flavored noodles are the ideal accompaniment.

NUTRITIONAL INFORMATION

Calories ....398 Sugars 8g
Protein ....34g Fat 5g
Carbohydrate ...54g Saturates 1g

15 mins   30 mins

SERVES 4

INGREDIENTS

4 boneless chicken breasts (about
  4¼ oz/125 g each)

2 tbsp clear honey

1 tbsp dark soy sauce

1 tsp lemon zest, finely grated

1 tbsp lemon juice

salt and pepper

NOODLES

8 oz/225 g rice noodles

2 tsp sesame oil

1 tbsp sesame seeds

1 tsp lemon zest, finely grated

TO GARNISH

1 tbsp fresh chives, chopped

lemon zest, finely grated

1 Preheat the broiler to medium. Skin and trim the chicken breasts to remove any excess fat, then wash and pat them dry with absorbent paper towels. Using a sharp knife, score the chicken breasts with a criss-cross pattern on both sides (making sure that you do not cut all the way through the meat).

2 Mix together the honey, soy sauce, lemon zest, and juice in a small bowl, and then season well with black pepper.

3 Arrange the chicken breasts on the broiler rack so that they do not overlap and brush with half the honey mixture. Cook for 10 minutes, turn over, then brush with the remaining mixture. Cook for another 8–10 minutes, or until cooked through.

4 Meanwhile, prepare the noodles according to the instructions on the packet. Drain well and pile into a warm serving bowl. Mix the noodles with the sesame oil, sesame seeds, and the lemon zest. Season and keep warm.

5 Drain the chicken and serve with a small mound of noodles. Garnish the final arrangement with chopped chives and lemon zest.

VARIATION

For a different flavor, replace the lemon with orange or lime. If you prefer, serve the chicken with boiled rice or pasta, which you can flavor with sesame seeds and citrus zest in the same way.

Harlequin Chicken

This colorful dish will tempt the appetites of all the family. Toddlers enjoy the fun shapes of the multi-colored bell peppers

NUTRITIONAL INFORMATION

Calories 183	Sugar 8g	
Protein 24g	Fats 6g	
Carbohydrates 8g	Saturates 1g	

5 mins   25 mins

SERVES 4

INGREDIENTS

10 skinless, boneless chicken thighs

1 onion

1 each red, green, and yellow bell peppers

1 tbsp sunflower oil

14 oz/400 g can chopped tomatoes

2 tbsp chopped fresh parsley

pepper

whole-wheat bread and salad, to serve

1 Using a sharp knife, cut the chicken thighs into bitesized pieces.

2 Peel and thinly slice the onion. Halve and deseed the peppers and cut into small diamond shapes.

3 Heat the sunflower oil in a shallow pan, then quickly fry the chicken and onion until golden.

4 Add the peppers and cook for 2–3 minutes, then stir in the tomatoes and chopped fresh parsley, and season with pepper.

5 Cover the pan tightly and simmer for approximately 15 minutes, or until the chicken and vegetables are tender. Remove from the pan and serve the Harlequin Chicken hot with whole-wheat bread and a green salad.

COOK'S TIP

If you're making this dish for small children, the chicken can be finely chopped or ground first.

Chicken with Vermouth

The aromatic flavors of vermouth makes a good base for the sauce, and when partnered with refreshing grapes ensures a delicious meal.

NUTRITIONAL INFORMATION

Calories	271	Sugars	.........5g
Protein	........31g	Fat	..........4g
Carbohydrate	...22g	Saturates	......1g

10 mins   45 mins

SERVES 4

INGREDIENTS

4 x 6 oz/175 g part-boned chicken breasts, skinned

²⁄₃ cup dry white vermouth

²⁄₃ cup fresh chicken bouillon (see page 5)

2 shallots, sliced thinly

14 oz/400 g can artichoke hearts, drained and halved

4¼ oz/125 g seedless green grapes

1 tbsp cornstarch mixed with 1 tbsp water

salt and pepper

spinach leaves, to garnish

freshly cooked vegetables, to serve

1 Cook the chicken breasts in a heavy-based nonstick skillet for 2–3 minutes on each side until sealed. Drain on paper towels.

2 Rinse out the pan, then add the dry vermouth and bouillon. Bring to a boil and add the shallots and chicken.

3 Cover and simmer for 35 minutes. Season with salt and pepper according to taste.

4 Carefully stir in the artichokes and the grapes, and then heat through for 2–3 minutes.

5 Stir in the cornstarch mixture until thickened. Garnish the chicken with spinach leaves and serve with freshly cooked vegetables.

COOK'S TIP

Vermouth is a mixture of wines. It is fortified, and enriched with a secret blend of herbs and spices. It is available in sweet and dry forms. Dry white wine would make a suitable substitute in this recipe.

Cheesy Baked Chicken

Cheese and mustard, and a simple, crispy coating, make a delicious combination for this healthy dish containing lowfat ingredients.

NUTRITIONAL INFORMATION

Calories	225	Sugars	.........1g
Protein	........32g	Fat	...........7g
Carbohydrate	....9g	Saturates	......3g

5 mins   35 mins

SERVES 4

INGREDIENTS

1 tbsp low-fat milk

2 tbsp English mustard

generous ½ cup low-fat, sharp
   Cheddar cheese, grated

3 tbsp all-purpose flour

2 tbsp chopped fresh chives

4 skinless, boneless chicken breasts

TO SERVE

jacket potatoes and fresh vegetables

crisp salad

1 Mix together the milk and mustard in a bowl. Mix the cheese with the flour and chives on a plate.

2 Dip the chicken into the milk and mustard mixture, brushing with a pastry brush to coat evenly.

3 Dip the chicken breasts into the cheese mixture, pressing to coat them evenly all over.

4 Place on a cookie sheet and spoon any spare cheese coating on top.

5 Bake the chicken in a preheated oven, at 400°F/200°C, for 30–35 minutes, or until golden brown and the juices run clear, not pink, when the chicken is pierced to the center with a skewer.

6 Serve the chicken hot, with jacket potatoes and fresh vegetables, or serve cold, with a crisp salad.

COOK'S TIP

Part-boned chicken breasts are very suitable for pan-cooking and casseroling, as they stay moist and tender. Try using chicken quarters if part-boned breasts are unavailable.

Fragrant Spiced Chicken

The combination of chicken and garbanzo beans is particularly tasty and nutritious. Use the canned variety for a quick meal.

NUTRITIONAL INFORMATION

Calories	343	Sugars	.........5g
Protein	........28g	Fat	..........16g
Carbohydrate	...24g	Saturates	......3g

10 mins   30 mins

SERVES 4

INGREDIENTS

3 tbsp ghee or vegetable oil

8 small chicken portions, such as thighs or drumsticks

1 large onion, peeled and chopped

2 garlic cloves, peeled and crushed

1–2 fresh green chiles, deseeded and chopped, or 1–2 tsp minced chilli (from a jar)

2 tsp ground cumin

2 tsp ground coriander

1 tsp garam masala

1 tsp ground turmeric

14 oz/400 g can chopped tomatoes

⅔ cup water

1 tbsp chopped fresh mint

14 oz/400 g can garbanzo beans, drained

salt

1 tbsp chopped fresh coriander

low-fat natural yogurt, to serve (optional)

1 Heat the ghee or oil in a large saucepan and fry the chicken until sealed all over and lightly golden.

2 Remove from the pan. Add the onion, garlic, chile, and spices and cook very gently for 2 minutes, stirring frequently.

3 Stir in the tomatoes, water, mint, and garbanzo beans. Mix thoroughly, return the chicken portions to the pan, season with salt, then cover and simmer gently for about 20 minutes, or until the chicken is tender.

4 Taste and adjust the seasoning, then sprinkle with the cilantro, and serve hot with yogurt, if using.

VARIATION

Canned black-eye peas and red kidney beans also make delicious additions to this spicy chicken dish. Be sure to drain and rinse canned beans before adding to the pan.

Chicken & Chili Bean Pot

This aromatic chicken dish has a spicy Mexican kick. Chicken thighs have a wonderful flavor when cooked in this Latin American way.

NUTRITIONAL INFORMATION

Calories	333	Sugars	........10g
Protein	........25g	Fat	..........13g
Carbohydrate	...32g	Saturates	......2g

🌣 🌣

🍲 10 mins   ⏱ 40 mins

SERVES 4

INGREDIENTS

2 tbsp all-purpose flour

1 tsp chili powder

8 chicken thighs or 4 chicken legs

3 tbsp vegetable oil

2 garlic cloves, crushed

1 large onion, chopped

1 green or red bell pepper, deseeded and chopped

1¼ cups chicken bouillon

12 oz/350 g tomatoes, chopped

14 oz/400 g can red kidney beans, rinsed and drained

2 tbsp tomato paste

salt and pepper

COOK'S TIP

For extra intensity of flavor, use sun-dried tomato paste instead of ordinary tomato paste.

1 Mix together the flour, chili powder, and seasoning in a shallow dish. Rinse the chicken, then dip into the seasoned flour, turning to coat it on all sides.

2 Heat the oil in a skillet or pan, add the chicken, and brown for 3–4 minutes evenly on all sides.

3 Lift the chicken out of the pan with a perforated spoon and drain.

4 Add the garlic, onion, and pepper to the pan and cook for 2–3 minutes, or until softened.

5 Add the bouillon, tomatoes, kidney beans, and tomato paste, stirring well. Bring to the boil, then return the chicken to the pan. Reduce the heat and simmer, covered, for about 30 minutes, or until the chicken is tender. Season and serve the bean pot at once while still hot.

Lemon & Tarragon Squab

Spatchcocked squab, or baby chickens, are complemented by the delicate fragrance of lemon and tarragon.

NUTRITIONAL INFORMATION

Calories 449	Sugars 2g
Protein 38g	Fat 30g
Carbohydrate 5g	Saturates 10g

15 mins   35 mins

SERVES 2

INGREDIENTS

2 squabs

4 sprigs fresh tarragon

1 tsp oil

2 tbsp butter

½ lemon zest

1 tbsp lemon juice

1 garlic clove, crushed

salt and pepper

tarragon and orange slices, to garnish

1 Prepare the squab, turn them breast-side down on a chopping board and cut them through the backbone using kitchen scissors. Crush each bird gently to break the bones so that they lie flat while cooking. Season each with salt.

2 Turn them over and insert a sprig of tarragon under the skin over each side of the breast.

3 Brush the chickens with oil, using a pastry brush, and place under a preheated hot broiler about 5 inches/ 13 cm from the heat. Broil the chickens for about 15 minutes, turning half way, until they are lightly browned.

4 To make the glaze, melt the butter in a saucepan, add the lemon zest and juice and garlic and season to taste.

5 Brush the squab with the glaze and cook for another 15 minutes, turning them once and brushing regularly so that they stay moist. Garnish the chickens with tarragon and orange slices and serve with new potatoes.

COOK'S TIP
Once the squab are flattened, insert 2 metal skewers through them to keep them flat.

Devilled Chicken

This succulent chicken is spiked with cayenne pepper and paprika, and finished off with a fruity, tangy sauce.

NUTRITIONAL INFORMATION

Calories 455   Sugars 19g
Protein . . . . .37g   Fat 23g
Carbohydrate . . .29g   Saturates 14g

🍲 10 mins   🕐 35 mins

SERVES 2–3

I N G R E D I E N T S

¼ cup all-purpose flour

1 tbsp cayenne pepper

1 tsp paprika

12 oz/350 g skinless, boneless
    chicken, diced

2 tbsp butter

1 onion, chopped finely

2 cups milk, warmed

4 tbsp applesauce

4¼ oz/125 g green grapes

⅔ cup sour cream

sprinkle of paprika

COOK'S TIP
Add more paprika if desired –
as it is quite a mild spice, you
can add plenty without it being
too overpowering.

1 Mix the flour, cayenne pepper, and paprika together and use the mixture to coat the chicken.

2 Shake off any excess flour. Melt the butter in a saucepan and gently fry the chicken with the onion for 4 minutes.

3 Stir in the flour and spice mixture. Add the milk slowly until thickened.

4 Simmer gently over a low heat until the sauce is smooth.

5 Add the applesauce and grapes and simmer gently for 20 minutes.

6 Transfer the chicken and devilled sauce to a serving dish and top with sour cream and a sprinkling of paprika.

Golden Chicken Pilau

This is a simple version of a creamy and mildly spiced Indian pilau. There are many ingredients, but very little preparation needed for this dish.

NUTRITIONAL INFORMATION

Calories 581	Sugars 22g	
Protein 31g	Fat 19g	
Carbohydrate . . .73g	Saturates 12g	

10 mins

20 mins

SERVES 4

I N G R E D I E N T S

4 tbsp butter

8 skinless, boneless chicken thighs, cut into large pieces

1 onion, sliced

1 tsp ground turmeric

1 tsp ground cinnamon

9 oz/250 g long-grain rice

1¾ cups unsweetened yogurt

2¼ oz/60 g golden raisins

¾ cup chicken bouillon

1 tomato, chopped

2 tbsp chopped fresh cilantro or parsley

2 tbsp coconut, toasted

salt and pepper

fresh cilantro, to garnish

1 Heat the butter in a heavy or nonstick skillet and fry the chicken with the onion for about 3 minutes.

2 Stir in the turmeric, cinnamon, rice, and seasoning and fry gently for 3 minutes.

3 Add the unsweetened yogurt, raisins, and chicken bouillon and mix well. Cover and simmer for 10 minutes, stirring occasionally until the rice is tender and all the chicken bouillon has been absorbed. Add more bouillon if the mixture starts to become too dry.

4 Stir in the chopped tomato and fresh cilantro or parsley. Season to taste.

5 Sprinkle the Golden Chicken Pilau with the toasted coconut and garnish with fresh cilantro.

COOK'S TIP

Long-grain rice is the most widely available and the cheapest rice. Basmati, with its slender grains and aromatic flavor, is more expensive. All rice, especially basmati, should be washed thoroughly under cold, running water before use.

Chicken & Chinese Cabbage

The great thing about stir-fries is you can cook with very little fat and still get lots of flavor, as in this light, healthy lunch dish.

NUTRITIONAL INFORMATION

Calories	329	Sugars	.........3g
Protein	........25g	Fat	...........4g
Carbohydrate	...46g	Saturates	.......1g

🍗 15 mins   🕐 25 mins

SERVES 4

INGREDIENTS

7 oz/200 g rice stick noodles

1 tbsp sunflower oil

1 garlic clove, finely chopped

¾ inch/2 cm piece fresh ginger, finely chopped

4 scallions, chopped

1 red bird-eye chile, deseeded and sliced

10½ oz/300 g boneless, skinless chicken, finely chopped

2 chicken livers, finely chopped

1 celery stalk, thinly sliced

1 carrot, cut into fine matchsticks

10½ oz/300 g shredded Chinese cabbage

4 tbsp lime juice

2 tbsp Thai fish sauce

1 tbsp soy sauce

TO GARNISH

2 tbsp fresh mint, shredded

slices of pickled garlic

fresh mint sprig

1 Soak the rice noodles in hot water for 15 minutes, or according to the package directions. Drain well.

2 Heat the oil in a wok or large killet and stir-fry the garlic, ginger, scallions, and chile for about 1 minute. Stir in the chicken and chicken livers, then stir-fry over a high heat for 2–3 minutes, or until beginning to brown.

3 Stir in the celery and carrot and stir-fry for 2 minutes to soften. Add the Chinese cabbage, then stir in the lime juice, fish sauce, and soy sauce.

4 Add the noodles and stir to heat thoroughly. Sprinkle with shredded mint and pickled garlic. Serve immediately, garnished with a mint sprig.

Chicken Tacos from Puebla

Seasoned chicken fills these soft tacos, along with creamy refried beans, avocado, smoky chipotle, and sour cream. It is a feast of tastes.

NUTRITIONAL INFORMATION

Calories	674	Sugars	........6g
Protein	........34g	Fat	..........25g
Carbohydrate	...80g	Saturates	.......9g

10 mins   5 mins

SERVES 4

I N G R E D I E N T S

8 corn tortillas

2 tsp vegetable oil

8–12 oz/225–350 g leftover cooked
  chicken, diced or shredded

8 oz/225 g can refried beans, warmed
  with 2 tbsp water to thin

¼ tsp ground cumin

¼ tsp dried oregano

1 avocado, pitted, sliced, and tossed
  with lime juice

salsa verde or salsa of your choice

1 canned chipotle chili in adobo marinade,
  chopped, or bottled chipotle salsa

¾ cup sour cream

½ onion, chopped

handful of lettuce leaves

5 radishes, diced

salt and pepper

1 Heat the tortillas for a few seconds each in an ungreased nonstick skillet in a stack, alternating the top and bottom tortillas so that the tortillas heat evenly. Wrap in kitchen foil or a clean dish cloth to keep warm.

2 Heat the oil in a skillet, add the diced or shredded chicken and heat through. Season with salt and pepper according to taste.

3 Thoroughly combine the refried beans with the cumin and oregano.

4 Spread one tortilla with warm refried beans, then top with a spoonful of the chicken, a slice or two of avocado, a dab of salsa, chipotle to taste, a dollop of sour cream, and a sprinkling of onion, lettuce, and radishes. Season with salt and pepper according to taste, then roll up, as tightly as you can. Repeat with the remaining tortillas and serve at once.

VARIATION

Replace the chicken with
1 lb/450 g ground beef browned
with a seasoning of chopped
onion, mild chili powder and
ground cumin to taste.

Green Chili Chilaquiles

Easy to put together, this dish makes a perfect midweek supper. Use tortilla chips instead of baking the tortillas, if you prefer.

NUTRITIONAL INFORMATION

Calories ....682 Sugars 1g
Protein ....60g Fat 38g
Carbohydrate ...26g Saturates 20g

15 mins   1 hr

SERVES 4–6

INGREDIENTS

12 stale tortillas, cut into strips

1 tbsp vegetable oil

1 small cooked chicken, meat removed from the bones and cut into bite-sized pieces

salsa verde

3 tbsp chopped fresh cilantro

1 tsp finely chopped fresh oregano or thyme

4 garlic cloves, finely chopped

¼ tsp ground cumin

12 oz/350 g grated cheese, such as Cheddar, manchego or mozzarella

16 fl oz/450 ml/2 cups chicken bouillon

4 oz/115 g Parmesan cheese, freshly grated

TO SERVE

1½ cups plain yogurt or sour cream

3–5 scallions, thinly sliced

pickled chilis

1 Place the tortilla strips in a roasting pan, toss with oil, then bake in a preheated oven, 375°F/190°C, for 30 minutes, or until they are golden.

2 Arrange the chicken in a 9 x 13 inch/ 23 x 33 cm casserole, then sprinkle with half the salsa, coriander, oregano, garlic, cumin, and some of the cheese. Repeat these layers and top with the tortilla strips.

3 Pour the bouillon over the top, then sprinkle with the remaining cheese.

4 Bake in a preheated oven at 375°F/190°C for about 30 minutes, or until heated through and the cheese is lightly golden in areas.

5 Serve garnished with the sour cream, sliced scallions, and pickled chilis to taste.

Potato & Banana Cakes

Potato cakes are usually served plain on the side. Here, they are combined with ground chicken and mashed banana for a fruit-flavored main course.

NUTRITIONAL INFORMATION

Calories . . . . . . .429 Sugars 11g
Protein . . . . .22g Fat 23g
Carbohydrate . . .39g Saturates 10g

15 mins   30 mins

SERVES 4

INGREDIENTS

1 lb/450 g mealy potatoes, diced

8 oz/225 g ground chicken

1 large banana

2 tbsp all-purpose flour

1 tsp lemon juice

1 onion, finely chopped

2 tbsp chopped fresh sage

2 tbsp butter

2 tbsp vegetable oil

⅔ cup light cream

⅔ cup chicken bouillon

salt and pepper

fresh sage leaves, to garnish

1 Cook the potatoes in boiling water for 10 minutes. Drain and mash the potatoes until smooth. Stir in the chicken.

2 Mash the banana and add it to the potato with the flour, lemon juice, onion, and half the chopped sage. Season well and stir the mixture together.

3 Divide the mixture into 8 equal portions. With lightly floured hands, shape each portion into a round patty.

4 Heat butter and oil in a skillet, then add the patties and cook for 12–15 minutes, turning once. Remove and keep warm.

5 Stir the cream and bouillon into the skillet with the remaining chopped sage. Cook over a low heat for 2–3 minutes.

6 Arrange the potato cakes on a serving plate, garnish with fresh sage leaves, and serve with the cream and sage sauce.

COOK'S TIP
Do not boil the sauce once the cream has been added as it will curdle. Cook it gently over a very low heat.

Golden Chicken Risotto

Long-grain rice can be used instead of risotto rice, but it will not give the traditional, creamy texture that is typical of Italian risottos.

NUTRITIONAL INFORMATION

Calories 701   Sugars 7g
Protein . . . . .35g   Fat 26g
Carbohydrate . . .88g   Saturates 8g

🍞 🍞

🍲 10 mins   🕙 30 mins

SERVES 4

INGREDIENTS

2 tbsp sunflower oil

1 tbsp butter or margarine

1 leek, thinly sliced

1 large yellow bell pepper, diced

3 skinless, boneless chicken breasts, diced

1¾ cups risotto rice

strands of saffron

7 cups chicken bouillon

7 oz/200 g can corn

2¼ oz/60 g unsalted peanuts, toasted

generous ½ cup Parmesan cheese, grated

salt and pepper

1 Heat oil and butter in a saucepan. Fry the leek and pepper for 1 minute, stir in the chicken and cook, stirring, until golden.

2 Stir in the risotto rice and cook for 2–3 minutes.

3 Stir in the saffron strands and salt and pepper. Add the chicken bouillon, a little at a time, then cover and cook over a low heat, stirring occasionally, for about 20 minutes, or until the rice is tender and most of the liquid has been absorbed. Do not let the risotto dry out – add more bouillon if necessary.

4 Stir in the corn, peanuts, and freshly-grated Parmesan cheese, then season with salt and pepper according to taste. Serve piping hot.

COOK'S TIP

Risottos can be frozen, before adding the Parmesan cheese, for up to 1 month, but remember to reheat this risotto thoroughly as it contains chicken.

Steamed Chicken Parcels

A healthy recipe with a delicate oriental flavor. Use large spinach leaves to wrap round the chicken, but make sure they are young leaves.

NUTRITIONAL INFORMATION

Calories . . . . .216 Sugars 7g
Protein . . . . .31g Fat 7g
Carbohydrate . . . .7g Saturates 2g

5 mins   30 mins

SERVES 4

INGREDIENTS

4 lean boneless, skinless chicken
  breasts

1 tsp ground lemon grass

2 scallions, chopped finely

9 oz/250 g young carrots

9 oz/250 g young zucchini

2 celery stalks

1 tsp light soy sauce

9 oz/250 g spinach leaves

2 tsp sesame oil

salt and pepper

1 With a sharp knife, make a slit through one side of each chicken breast, to open out a large pocket.

2 Sprinkle the inside of the pocket with lemon grass, salt, and pepper. Tuck the scallions into each of the chicken pockets.

3 Trim the carrots, zucchini, and celery, then cut into small matchsticks.

Plunge them into a pan of boiling water for 1 minute, then drain and toss in the soy sauce.

4 Pack the mixture into the pockets in each chicken breast and fold over firmly to enclose. Reserve the remaining vegetables. Wash and dry the spinach leaves, then wrap the chicken breasts firmly in the leaves to enclose completely. If the leaves are too firm, steam

them for a few seconds until they are softened and flexible.

5 Place the wrapped chicken in a steamer and steam over rapidly boiling water for 20–25 minutes, depending on size.

6 Stir-fry any leftover vegetable sticks and spinach for 1–2 minutes in the sesame oil and serve with the chicken.

Chicken with Cashew Nuts

This dish is popular dish with customers at Chinatown restaurants all over the West. It can taste even better if you make it yourself.

NUTRITIONAL INFORMATION

Calories 330   Sugars 5g
Protein ....22g   Fat 18g
Carbohydrate ...19g   Saturates 3g

10 mins, plus 20 mins to marinate   15 mins

SERVES 4

INGREDIENTS

10½ oz/300 g boneless, skinless chicken breasts

1 tbsp cornstarch

1 tsp sesame oil

1 tbsp hoisin sauce

1 tsp light soy sauce

3 garlic cloves, crushed

2 tbsp vegetable oil

2¾ oz/75 g unsalted cashew nuts

1 oz/25 g snow peas

1 celery stalk, sliced

1 onion, cut into 8 pieces

2¼ oz/60 g beansprouts

1 red bell pepper, deseeded and diced

SAUCE

2 tsp cornstarch

2 tbsp hoisin sauce

¾ cup chicken bouillon

1 Trim any fat from the chicken breasts and cut the meat into thin strips. Place the chicken in a large mixing bowl. Sprinkle with the cornstarch and toss to coat the chicken strips in it, shaking off any excess. Mix together the sesame oil, hoisin sauce, soy sauce, and 1 garlic clove. Pour this mixture over the chicken, turning to coat thoroughly. Let marinate for 20 minutes.

2 Heat half the vegetable oil in a preheated wok. Add the cashew nuts and stir-fry for 1 minute, or until browned. Add the snow peas, celery, the remaining garlic, the onion, beansprouts, and red pepper and cook, stirring occasionally, for 2–3 minutes. Remove the vegetables from the wok with a slotted spoon, set aside and keep warm.

3 Heat the remaining oil in the wok. Remove the chicken from the marinade and stir-fry for 3–4 minutes. Return the vegetables to the wok.

4 To make the sauce, mix the cornstarch, hoisin sauce, and chicken bouillon together and pour into the wok. Bring to the boil, stirring until thickened and clear. Serve immediately on warm serving plates.

Chicken Fu Yung

Although commonly described as an omelet, fu yung ("white lotus petals") uses only egg whites to create its very delicate texture.

NUTRITIONAL INFORMATION

Calories 220   Sugars 1g
Protein ....16g   Fat 14g
Carbohydrate ....7g   Saturates 3g

10 mins   5 mins

SERVES 4

I N G R E D I E N T S

6 oz/175 g chicken breast fillet, skinned

½ tsp salt

pepper

1 tsp rice wine or dry sherry

1 tbsp cornstarch

3 eggs

salt

½ tsp scallions, finely chopped

3 tbsp vegetable oil

4¼ oz/125 g green peas

1 tsp light soy sauce

drops of sesame oil

1 Cut the chicken across the grain into very small, paper-thin slices, using a cleaver. Place the chicken slices in a shallow dish.

2 In a small bowl, mix together ½ teaspoon salt, pepper, rice wine or dry sherry, and cornflour.

3 Pour the mixture over the chicken slices in the dish, turning the chicken until well coated.

4 Beat the eggs in a small bowl with a pinch of salt and the scallions.

5 Heat the vegetable oil in a preheated wok, then add the chicken slices and stir-fry for about 1 minute, making sure that the slices are kept separated.

6 Pour the beaten eggs over the chicken, and lightly scramble until set. Do not stir too vigorously, or the mixture will break up in the oil. Stir the oil from the bottom of the wok so that the fu yung rises to the surface.

7 Add the peas, light soy sauce, and salt to taste and blend well. Transfer to warm serving dishes, sprinkle with sesame oil and serve.

COOK'S TIP
If available, chicken goujons can be used for this dish: these are small, delicate strips of chicken which require no further cutting and are very tender.

Chicken Noodles

Rice noodles are used in this delicious recipe. They are available in large many large stores as well as in specialist Chinese stores.

NUTRITIONAL INFORMATION

Calories 169	Sugars 2g
Protein 14g	Fat 7g
Carbohydrate ...12g	Saturates 2g

5 mins   15 mins

SERVES 4

INGREDIENTS

8 oz/225 g rice noodles

2 tbsp peanut oil

8 oz/225 g skinless, boneless chicken breast, sliced

2 garlic cloves, crushed

1 tsp fresh ginger, grated

1 tsp Chinese curry powder

1 red bell pepper, deseeded and thinly sliced

2¾ oz/75 g snow peas, shredded

1 tbsp light soy sauce

2 tsp Chinese rice wine

2 tbsp chicken bouillon

1 tsp sesame oil

1 tbsp chopped fresh cilantro

VARIATION

For a tasty change, you can use pork or duck in this recipe instead of the chicken, if you prefer.

1 Soak the rice noodles for 4 minutes in warm water. Drain thoroughly and set aside until required.

2 Heat the peanut oil in a preheated wok or large heavy-based skillet and stir-fry the chicken slices for 2–3 minutes.

3 Add the garlic, ginger, and Chinese curry powder and stir-fry for another 30 seconds. Add the red pepper and snow peas to the mixture in the wok and stir-fry for 2–3 minutes.

4 Add the noodles, soy sauce, rice wine, and chicken bouillon and mix well, stirring occasionally, for 1 minute.

5 Sprinkle the sesame oil and chopped cilantro over the noodles. Transfer to serving plates and serve.

Chicken & Cheese Jackets

Use the breasts from a roasted chicken to make these delicious potatoes, and serve them as a light lunch or supper dish.

NUTRITIONAL INFORMATION

Calories 417   Sugars 4g
Protein . . . . .28g   Fat 10g
Carbohydrate . . .57g   Saturates 5g

5 mins   50 mins

SERVES 4

I N G R E D I E N T S

4 large baking potatoes

8 oz/225 g cooked, boneless
  chicken breasts

4 scallions

9 oz/250 g low-fat soft cheese
  or Quark

pepper

1 Scrub the baking potatoes and pat them dry thoroughly with absorbent paper towels.

2 Prick the potatoes all over with a fork. Bake in a preheated oven, 400°F/200°C/, for about 50 minutes until tender, or cook in a microwave on a high setting for 12–15 minutes.

3 Using a sharp knife, dice the chicken and trim and thickly slice the scallions. Place the chicken and scallions in a bowl.

4 Add the low-fat soft cheese or Quark to the chicken and scallions and stir well to combine.

5 Cut a cross through the top of each potato and pull slightly apart. Spoon the chicken filling into the potatoes, and sprinkle with pepper.

6 Serve the chicken and cheese jackets immediately with coleslaw, green salad, or a mixed salad.

COOK'S TIP
Look for Quark in the chilled section. It is a low-fat, white, fresh curd cheese made from cow's milk. It has a delicate, slightly sour flavor.

Chicken Jalfrezi

This is a quick and tasty way to use leftover roast chicken. The sauce can also be used for any cooked poultry, lamb, or beef.

NUTRITIONAL INFORMATION

Calories 270   Sugars 3g
Protein . . . . .36g   Fat 11g
Carbohydrate . . . .7g   Saturates 2g

15 mins   15 mins

SERVES 4

INGREDIENTS

1 tsp mustard oil

3 tbsp vegetable oil

1 large onion, chopped finely

3 garlic cloves, crushed

1 tbsp tomato paste

2 tomatoes, skinned and chopped

1 tsp ground turmeric

½ tsp cumin seeds, ground

½ tsp cilantro seeds, ground

½ tsp chili powder

½ tsp garam masala

1 tsp red wine vinegar

1 small red bell pepper, chopped

4¼ oz/125 g frozen fava beans

1 lb 2 oz/500 g cooked chicken, cut into bite-sized pieces

salt

sprigs of fresh cilantro, to garnish

1 Heat the mustard oil in a large, skillet set over a high heat for approximately 1 minute, or until the oil begins to smoke.

2 Add the vegetable oil, reduce the heat, and then add the onion and the garlic. Fry the garlic and onion until they are golden.

3 Add the tomato paste, chopped tomatoes, turmeric, ground cumin cilantro seeds, chili powder, garam masala, and wine vinegar to the skillet. Stir the mixture until fragrant.

4 Add the red pepper and fava beans and stir for 2 minutes, or until the pepper is softened. Stir in the chicken, and salt to taste.

5 Simmer gently for 6–8 minute, or until the chicken is heated through and the beans are tender.

6 Serve as soon after cooking as possible, garnished with sprigs of fresh cilantro.

Oriental Chicken Salad

Mirin (the Japanese sweet rice wine), soy sauce, and sesame oil give an oriental flavor to this delicious salad.

NUTRITIONAL INFORMATION

Calories	.361	Sugars	.2g
Protein	.34g	Fat	.16g
Carbohydrate	.17g	Saturates	.3g

10 mins   35 mins

SERVES 4

INGREDIENTS

4 skinless, boneless chicken breasts

⅓ scant cup mirin or sweet sherry

⅓ scant cup light soy sauce

1 tbsp sesame oil

3 tbsp olive oil

1 tbsp red wine vinegar

1 tbsp Dijon mustard

9 oz/250 g egg noodles

9 oz/250 g bean sprouts

9 oz/250 g Chinese cabbage, shredded

2 scallions, sliced

4¼ oz/125 g mushrooms, sliced

1 fresh red chile, finely sliced,
    to garnish

1 Pound the boneless chicken breasts out to an even thickness between two sheets of plastic wrap with a rolling pin or cleaver.

2 Put the chicken breasts in a roasting pan. Combine the mirin and soy sauce and brush over the chicken.

3 Place the chicken in a preheated oven, 400°F/200°C, for 20–30 minutes, basting often.

4 Remove the chicken from the oven and let cool slightly.

5 Combine the sesame oil, olive oil, and red wine vinegar with the mustard.

6 Cook the noodles according to the instructions on the packet. Rinse under cold running water, then drain.

7 Toss the noodles in the dressing until the noodles are completely coated.

8 Toss the bean sprouts, Chinese cabbage, scallions, and mushrooms together with the noodles.

9 Slice the cooked chicken very thinly and stir into the noodles. Garnish the salad with the chile slices, and serve.

Chicken Pan Bagna

Perfect for a picnic, this Mediterranean-style sandwich can be prepared in very little time and in advance.

NUTRITIONAL INFORMATION

Calories 366   Sugars 2g
Protein . . . . .20g   Fat 23g
Carbohydrate . . .20g   Saturates 4g

🥪 5 mins   🕐 0 mins

SERVES 6

INGREDIENTS

1 large French stick

1 garlic clove

½ cup good quality olive oil

¾ oz/20 g canned anchovy fillets

1¾ oz/50 g cold roast chicken

2 large tomatoes, sliced

8 large, pitted black olives, chopped

pepper

1 Using a sharp bread knife, cut the French stick in half lengthwise and open it out flat.

2 Cut the garlic clove in half and rub it liberally over the bread.

3 Sprinkle the cut surface of the garlic-flavored bread lightly with the olive oil, and leave to soak in.

4 Drain the canned anchovies and set aside temporarily.

5 Thinly slice the chicken and arrange on top of the bread. Arrange the tomatoes and anchovies on top of the chicken.

6 Scatter with the olives and pepper. Sandwich the loaf back together and wrap in foil before serving in slices.

VARIATION

You could use Italian ciabatta or olive-studded focaccia bread instead of the French stick, if you prefer.

Coronation Chicken

This classic salad is good as a starter or as part of a buffet. Mango chutney makes a tasty accompaniment.

NUTRITIONAL INFORMATION

Calories	660	Sugars	.........5g
Protein	........40g	Fat	..........53g
Carbohydrate	....7g	Saturates	.......9g

10 mins   15 mins

SERVES 6

I N G R E D I E N T S

4 tbsp olive oil

2 lb/900 g chicken, diced

4¼ oz/125 g rindless, smoked
  bacon, diced

12 shallots

2 garlic cloves, crushed

1 tbsp mild curry powder

2½ cups mayonnaise

1 tbsp runny honey

1 tbsp chopped fresh parsley

pepper

3¼ oz/90 g seedless black grapes,
  quartered

cold saffron rice, to serve

1 Heat the oil in a large skillet and add the chicken, bacon, shallots, garlic, and curry powder. Cook slowly for about 15 minutes.

2 Spoon the cooked mixture into a clean mixing bowl.

3 Let the mixture cool completely before seasoning with pepper according to taste.

4 Blend the mayonnaise with a little honey, then add the chopped fresh parsley. Toss the chicken in the mixture.

5 Place the mixture in a deep serving dish, then garnish with the grapes. Serve with cold saffron rice.

VARIATION
You can use this recipe to fill a jacket potato or sandwich. Cut the chicken into smaller pieces.

Indonesian Chicken Salad

The spicy peanut dressing served with this salad may be prepared in advance and left to chill a day before required.

NUTRITIONAL INFORMATION

Calories 802   Sugars 15g
Protein ....35g   Fat 55g
Carbohydrate ...45g   Saturates 10g

15 mins   10 mins

SERVES 4

INGREDIENTS

4 large waxy potatoes, diced

10½ oz/300 g fresh pineapple, diced

2 carrots, grated

6 oz/175 g beansprouts

1 bunch scallions, sliced

1 large zucchini, cut into matchsticks

3 celery stalks, cut into matchsticks

6 oz/175 g unsalted peanuts

2 cooked chicken breast fillets (about 4¼ oz/125 g each), sliced

DRESSING

6 tbsp crunchy peanut butter

6 tbsp olive oil

2 tbsp light soy sauce

1 red chile, chopped

2 tsp sesame oil

4 tsp lime juice

COOK'S TIP

Unsweetened canned pineapple may be used in place of the fresh pineapple for convenience. If only sweetened, canned pineapple is available, drain it and rinse under cold running water before using.

1 Cook the diced potatoes in a saucepan of boiling water for 10 minutes or until tender. Drain and let cool.

2 Transfer the cooled potatoes to a salad bowl.

3 Add the pineapple, carrots, beansprouts, scallions, zucchini, celery, peanuts, and sliced chicken to the potatoes. Toss well to mix.

4 To make the dressing, put the peanut butter in a small bowl and gradually whisk in the olive oil and light soy sauce.

5 Stir in the chopped red chile, sesame oil, and lime juice. Mix well.

6 Pour the spicy dressing over the salad and toss lightly to coat all of the ingredients. Serve the salad immediately, garnished with the lime wedges.

Spicy Chicken Salad

Tender chicken breast meat cut into small pieces is perfect for salads. The chicken pieces cook quickly and can be tossed with other salad ingredients.

NUTRITIONAL INFORMATION

Calories 259	Sugars 9g
Protein 18g	Fat 12g
Carbohydrate ...22g	Saturates 5g

10 mins   25 mins

SERVES 4

INGREDIENTS

2 skinned chicken breast fillets (about 4¼ oz/125 g each)

2 tbsp butter

1 red chile, chopped

1 tbsp clear honey

½ tsp ground cumin

2 tbsp chopped fresh cilantro

2 large potatoes, diced

1¾ oz/50 g thin green beans, halved

1 red bell pepper, cut into thin strips

2 tomatoes, deseeded and diced

DRESSING

2 tbsp olive oil

pinch of chili powder

1 tbsp garlic wine vinegar

pinch of superfine sugar

1 tbsp chopped fresh cilantro

1 Cut the chicken breast fillets into thin strips using a sharp knife. Melt the butter in a medium-sized saucepan over a medium heat and then add the chicken, chile, honey, and cumin. Cook together for approximately 10 minutes, turning until cooked through.

2 Transfer the cooked mixture to a clean bowl. Let cool and then stir in the cilantro.

3 Meanwhile, cook the diced potatoes in a saucepan of boiling water for 10 minutes, or until tender. Drain and let cool.

4 Blanch the halved, thin green beans in a saucepan full of boiling water for 3 minutes. Drain the beans thoroughly and put them to one side to cool. Mix the green beans and potatoes together in a salad bowl.

5 Add the pepper strips and diced tomatoes to the potatoes and beans. Stir in the spicy chicken mixture.

6 In a small bowl, whisk the dressing ingredients together and pour the dressing over the salad, tossing well. Serve at once.

Pasta & Chicken Medley

Strips of cooked chicken are tossed with colored pasta, grapes, and carrot sticks in a Mediterranean-style pesto-flavored dressing.

NUTRITIONAL INFORMATION

Calories	.609	Sugars	11g
Protein	26g	Fat	38g
Carbohydrate	45g	Saturates	6g

20 mins   10 mins

SERVES 2

FRENCH DRESSING

1 tbsp wine vinegar

3 tbsp extra-virgin olive oil

salt and pepper

INGREDIENTS

4¼–5½ oz/125–150 g dried pasta shapes, such as twists or bows

1 tbsp oil

2 tbsp mayonnaise

2 tsp bottled pesto sauce

1 tbsp sour cream or plain, unsweetened yogurt

6 oz/175 g cooked skinless, boneless chicken

1–2 celery stalks

4½ oz/125 g black grapes (preferably seedless)

1 large carrot, trimmed

salt and pepper

celery leaves, to garnish

1 To make the French dressing, whisk all the ingredients together until they are evenly blended.

2 Cook the pasta with the oil for 8–10 minutes in boiling, salted water until tender. Drain, rinse, then drain again. Transfer to a bowl and mix in 1 tablespoon of dressing while hot; set aside until cold.

3 Combine the mayonnaise, pesto sauce, and sour cream or yogurt in a clean bowl, and season with salt and pepper according to taste.

4 Cut the chicken into narrow strips. Cut the celery diagonally into narrow slices. Reserve a few grapes for garnish, halve the rest, and remove any pips. Cut the carrot into narrow julienne strips.

5 Add the chicken, the celery, the halved grapes, the carrot, and the mayonnaise mixture to the pasta, and toss thoroughly. Check the seasoning, adding more salt and pepper if necessary.

6 Arrange the pasta mixture on two plates and garnish with the reserved black grapes and the celery leaves.

Chargrilled Chicken Salad

This is a quick starter to serve at a barbecue. If the bread is folded in half, the chicken salad can be put in the middle and eaten as finger food.

NUTRITIONAL INFORMATION

Calories ....225 Sugars 5g
Protein ....16g Fat 12g
Carbohydrate ...15g Saturates 2g

10 mins   15 mins

SERVES 4

INGREDIENTS

2 skinless, boneless chicken breasts

1 red onion

oil for brushing

1 avocado, peeled and pitted

1 tbsp lemon juice

½ cup low-fat mayonnaise

¼ tsp chili powder

½ tsp pepper

¼ tsp salt

4 tomatoes, quartered

½ loaf sun-dried tomato-flavored focaccia bread

green salad, to serve

1 Using a sharp knife, cut the chicken breasts into ½ inch/1 cm strips.

2 Cut the onion into eight pieces, held together at the root. Rinse under cold running water and then brush with oil.

3 Purée or mash the avocado and lemon juice together. Whisk in the mayonnaise. Add the chili powder, pepper, and salt.

4 Put the chicken and onion over a hot barbecue and broil for 3–4 minutes on each side. Combine the chicken, onion, tomatoes, and avocado mixture together.

5 Cut the bread in half twice, so that you have quarter-circle shaped pieces, then in half horizontally. Toast on the barbeque for about 2 minutes on each side.

6 Spoon the chicken mixture on to the toasts, and serve with a green salad.

VARIATION

Instead of focaccia, serve the salad in pitta breads which have been warmed through on the barbecue.

Spinach Salad

Fresh baby spinach is tasty and light, and it makes an excellent salad to go with the chicken and the creamy, orange-flavored dressing.

NUTRITIONAL INFORMATION

Calories 145	Sugars 3g
Protein 10g	Fat 10g
Carbohydrate 4g	Saturates 1g

15 mins   0 mins

SERVES 4

INGREDIENTS

1¾ oz/50 g mushrooms

3½ oz/100 g baby spinach, washed

2¾ oz/75 g radicchio leaves, shredded

3½ oz/100 g cooked chicken breast

1¾ oz/50 g prosciutto

DRESSING

2 tbsp olive oil

½ orange, finely grated zest and 1 orange, juiced

1 tbsp unsweetened yogurt

1 Wipe the mushrooms with a damp cloth to remove any excess dirt.

2 Gently mix together the spinach and radicchio in a large salad bowl.

3 Using a sharp knife, thinly slice the wiped mushrooms and add them to the bowl containing the baby spinach and radicchio leaves, ready for the addition of the other salad ingredients.

4 Tear the cooked chicken breast and prosciutto into strips with the your hands and mix them thoroughly into the spinach salad.

5 To make the dressing, place the olive oil, orange zest, juice, and yogurt into a screw-top jar. Shake the jar until the mixture is well combined. Season to taste with salt and pepper.

6 Drizzle the dressing over the spinach salad and toss to mix well. Serve.

VARIATION

Spinach is delicious when served raw. Try raw spinach in a salad garnished with bacon or garlicky croûtons. The young leaves have a wonderfully sharp flavor.

Chinese Chicken Salad

This is a refreshing dish suitable for a summer meal or a light lunch. It is a healthy dish, composed of fresh vegetables and low in fat.

NUTRITIONAL INFORMATION

Calories 162   Sugars 3g
Protein . . . . .15g   Fat 10g
Carbohydrate . . . .5g   Saturates 2g

20 mins, plus 20 mins to marinate   10 mins

SERVES 4

INGREDIENTS

8 oz/225 g skinless, boneless
   chicken breasts

2 tsp light soy sauce

1 tsp sesame oil

1 tsp sesame seeds

2 tbsp vegetable oil

4¼ oz/125 g bean sprouts

1 red bell pepper, deseeded and thinly sliced

1 carrot, cut into matchsticks

3 baby corn cobs, sliced

snipped chives and carrot matchsticks,
   to garnish

SAUCE

2 tsp rice wine vinegar

1 tbsp light soy sauce

dash of chili oil

1 Place the chicken breasts in a shallow glass dish.

2 Mix together the soy sauce and sesame oil and pour over the chicken. Sprinkle with the sesame seeds and let stand for 20 minutes, turning the chicken over occasionally.

3 Remove the chicken from the marinade and cut the meat into thin slices using a sharp knife.

4 Heat the vegetable oil in a preheated wok or large skillet. Add the chicken and fry for 4–5 minutes, or until cooked through and golden brown on both sides. Remove the chicken from the wok with a slotted spoon, then set aside and let cool.

5 Add the bean sprouts, pepper, carrot, and baby corn cobs to the wok and stir-fry for 2–3 minutes. Remove from the wok with a slotted spoon, then set aside and let cool.

6 For the sauce, mix the rice wine vinegar, light soy sauce, and chili oil.

7 Arrange the chicken and vegetables on a serving plate. Spoon over the sauce and garnish with chives and carrots.

Layered Chicken Salad

This layered main-course salad has lively tastes and textures. For an interesting variation, substitute canned tuna for the chicken.

NUTRITIONAL INFORMATION

Calories 352	Sugars 9g
Protein 29g	Fat 9g
Carbohydrate ...43g	Saturates 2g

20 mins   40 mins

SERVES 4

INGREDIENTS

1 lb 10 oz/750 g new potatoes, scrubbed

1 red bell pepper, halved, cored, and deseeded

1 green pepper, halved, cored, and deseeded

2 small zucchini, sliced

1 small onion, thinly sliced

3 tomatoes, sliced

12 oz/350 g cooked chicken, sliced

snipped fresh chives, to garnish

YOGURT DRESSING

5½ oz/150 g low-fat unsweetened yogurt

3 tbsp low-fat mayonnaise

1 tbsp snipped fresh chives

salt and pepper

1 Place the new potatoes into a large saucepan of cold water. Bring to the boil, then reduce the heat. Cover the saucepan and simmer for 15–20 minutes, or until tender.

2 Meanwhile place the pepper halves, cut side down, under a preheated hot broiler and broil until the skins blacken and begin to char.

3 Remove the peppers and let cool, then peel off the skins and slice the flesh. Set to one side.

4 Cook the zucchini in a small amount of lightly salted boiling water for 3 minutes.

5 Rinse the zucchini with cold water to cool quickly and set aside.

6 To make the dressing, mix the yogurt, mayonnaise, and snipped chives together in a small bowl. Season well with salt and pepper.

7 Drain, cool, then slice the potatoes. Add them to the dressing and mix well to coat evenly. Divide between 4 individual serving plates.

8 Top each plate with one quarter of the pepper slices and cooked zucchini. Layer one quarter of the onion and tomato slices, then the sliced chicken, on top of each serving. Garnish with snipped fresh chives and serve.

Chicken & Grape Salad

Tender chicken breast, sweet grapes, and crisp celery coated in a mild curry mayonnaise make a wonderful al fresco lunch.

NUTRITIONAL INFORMATION

Calories 413   Sugars 20g
Protein . . . . .39g   Fat 20g
Carbohydrate . . .20g   Saturates 3g

15 mins   0 mins

SERVES 4

I N G R E D I E N T S

1 lb 2 oz/500 g cooked skinless, boneless
  chicken breasts

2 celery stalks, sliced finely

9 oz/250 g black grapes

generous ½ cup split almonds, toasted

pinch of paprika

sprigs of fresh cilantro or
  flatleaf parsley, to garnish

C U R R Y   S A U C E

⅔ cup low-fat mayonnaise

4¼ oz/125 g unsweetened low-fat yogurt

1 tbsp clear honey

1 tbsp curry paste

1 Cut the chicken into fairly large pieces and transfer to a bowl with the sliced celery.

2 Halve the grapes, remove the pips, and add to the bowl.

3 To make the curry sauce, mix carefully together the mayonnaise, fromage frais, honey, and curry paste together until blended.

4 Pour the curry sauce over the salad and mix together carefully until thoroughly coated.

5 Transfer to a shallow serving dish and sprinkle with the split almonds and paprika.

6 Garnish the salad with the cilantro or parsley.

COOK'S TIP
To save time, use seedless grapes, now widely available in supermarkets, and add them whole to the salad.

Waldorf Chicken Salad

This colorful and healthy dish is a variation of a classic salad. You can use a selection of mixed salad leaves as an alternative.

NUTRITIONAL INFORMATION

Calories 471	Sugars 19g
Protein 38g	Fat 27g
Carbohydrate . . .20g	Saturates 4g

15 , plus
40 mins to marinate   45 mins

SERVES 4

INGREDIENTS

1 lb 2 oz/500 g red apples, diced

3 tbsp fresh lemon juice

⅔ cup low-fat mayonnaise

1 head of celery

4 shallots, sliced

1 garlic clove, crushed

¾ cup walnuts, chopped

1 lb 2 oz/500 g lean cooked chicken, cubed

1 romaine lettuce

pepper

sliced apple and walnuts, to garnish

VARIATION

Instead of the shallots, use scallions for a milder flavor. Trim the scallions and slice finely.

1 Place the apples in a bowl with the lemon juice and 1 tablespoon of mayonnaise. Set aside for at least 40 minutes, or until required.

2 Slice the head of celery very thinly. Add the celery together with the shallots, garlic, and walnuts to the coated apples and mix them well, then add the remaining mayonnaise before blending thoroughly.

3 Add the chicken and mix with the other ingredients.

4 Line a glass salad bowl or serving dish with the lettuce.

5 Pile the chicken salad into the center, sprinkle with pepper, then garnish with apple slices and walnuts.

Old English Spicy Salad

This is an excellent recipe for leftover roast chicken. Add the dressing just before serving, so the spinach retains its crispness.

NUTRITIONAL INFORMATION

Calories . . . . . . .225 Sugars 4g
Protein . . . . .25g Fat 12g
Carbohydrate . . . .4g Saturates 2g

🥗 10 mins 🕐 0 mins

SERVES 4

INGREDIENTS

8 oz/225 g young spinach leaves

3 celery stalks, sliced thinly

½ cucumber, sliced thinly

2 scallions, sliced thinly

3 tbsp chopped fresh parsley

12 oz/350g boneless, lean roast chicken, sliced thinly

DRESSING

1 inch/2.5 cm piece fresh ginger, grated finely

3 tbsp olive oil

1 tbsp white wine vinegar

1 tbsp clear honey

½ tsp ground cinnamon

salt and pepper

smoked almonds, to garnish (optional)

1 Thoroughly wash and dry the young spinach leaves.

2 Toss the celery, cucumber, and scallions with the spinach and parsley in a large bowl.

3 Transfer the salad ingredients to serving plates and arrange the chicken over the salad.

4 To make the dressing, combine the grated ginger, olive oil, wine vinegar, honey, and cinnamon in a screw-topped jar and shake well to mix. Season with salt and pepper to taste.

5 Pour the dressing over the salad. Scatter a few smoked almonds over the salad to garnish, if using.

COOK'S TIP

For extra color, add some cherry tomatoes and some thin strips of red and yellow peppers and garnish with a little grated carrot.

This is a Parragon Publishing Book
This edition published in 2003

Parragon Publishing
Queen Street House
4 Queen Street
Bath BA1 1HE, UK

Copyright © Parragon 2001

All rights reserved. No part of this publication may be reproduced, stored
in a retrieval system or transmitted, in any form or by any means, electronic,
mechanical, photocopying, recording or otherwise, without the prior permission
of the copyright holder.

ISBN: 1-40540-873-1

Printed in China

NOTE

This book uses metric and imperial measurements. Follow the same units
of measurement throughout; do not mix metric and imperial.
All spoon measurements are level: teaspoons are assumed to be 5 ml, and
tablespoons are assumed to be 15 ml. Unless otherwise stated,
milk is assumed to be full fat, eggs and individual vegetables such as potatoes
are medium, and pepper is freshly ground black pepper.

The nutritional information provided for each recipe is per serving or per person.
Optional ingredients, variations or serving suggestions have
not been included in the calculations. The times given for each recipe are an approximate
guide only because the preparation times may differ according to the techniques used by
different people and the cooking times may vary as a result of the type of oven used.

Recipes using raw or very lightly cooked eggs should be
avoided by infants, the elderly, pregnant women, convalescents,
and anyone suffering from an illness.

The publisher would like to thank
Steamer Trading Cookshop, Lewes, East Sussex, for the kind loan of props.